W9-CFI-903

WHOLE PARENT WHOLE CHILD

WHOLE PARENT WHOLE CHILD

A Parents' Guide to Raising A Child With A Chronic Illness

**PATRICIA M. MOYNIHAN, R.N. P.N.P., M.P.H.
& BROATCH HAIG, R.D., C.D.E.**

Whole Parent, Whole Child. Copyright 1989 by
Patricia Moynihan, R.N.,P.N.P.,M.P.H.,
Broatch Haig, R.D.,C.D.E.

All rights reserved. Except for brief passages used for review purposes, no part of this publication may be reproduced, stored in a re-
trieval system or transmitted, in any form or by any means, elec-
tronic, mechanical, photocopying, recording, or otherwise, without
the prior written permission of DCI Publishing, Inc.

Library of Congress Cataloging-in-Publication Data
Moynihan, Patricia.
    Whole parent, whole child.
    (The Wellness series)
    Bibliography: p. 177
    Includes index.
    1. Chronically ill children. 2. Child rearing.
I. Haig, Broatch. II. Title. III. Series.
RJ380.M68 1988   649'.8   88-30988
ISBN 0-937721-53-0

Edited by: Donna Hoel
Cover & Text Design: Terry Dugan Design
Production Manager: Wenda Johnson
Printed in the United States of America

10 9 8 7 6 5 4 3 2 1

Published by:
DCI Publishing, Inc.
P.O. Box 739
Wayzata, Minnesota 55391

Contents

Acknowledgments

· ·

The creation of this book involved the work, patience, thoughtful review, and steadfast encouragement of many people. We don't have the space to list each and every one, but we do want to extend special thanks to the following special people.

• Martha Spencer, M.D., and Joseph Nelson, M.A., L.P., for their in-depth and sensitive review of the manuscript.

• Donnell Etzwiler, M.D., for his visionary leadership.

• Doug Toft for editing the manuscript and for special assistance with expanding the focus from Diabetes to chronic illness.

• Donna Hoel and Pat Richter for editing revisions, typing the manuscript, and preparing the index.

• Barbara Balik, R.N., M.S., for support and encouragement in developing the concept of positive parenting.

• Georgianna Larson, R.N., P.N.P., M.P.H., for assistance in research on chronic illness and available resources.

• Donald Brunnquelle, Ph.D., for help with research.

• Judith, Eugene, and Mark Bennett and Marlene, Norm, Cindee, and Lynnette Miller for sharing their thoughts about living with chronic illness.

• Services for Children with Handicaps, Minnesota Department of Health, for their support of parents, families, and the Minnesota Diabetes in Youth Program.

• All the children and families working with the Minnesota Diabetes in Youth Program, for their insights into the meaning of chronic illness. Our respect for them moved us to write this book.

• The entire staff of the International Diabetes Center for their never-failing support and encouragement.

• B.C. Gamble and P.W. Skogmo Foundation for the generous grant that made development of this book possible.

Introduction

· ·

What kind of parent are you now?

What kind of parent do you want to be?

And how can you help your child with chronic illness lead the fullest life?

Those are the three questions behind every word in this book. In these pages you'll find answers to these questions and – we hope – some practical suggestions that will really work for you.

Raising a child is a constant challenge, stress, wonder, exhaustion, joy – all at once. And when your child has a chronic illness, each of these factors gains intensity. Faced with this fact, many parents of such children feel desperate, even lonely. Though they may never say so, the same phrases run through their heads, echoing a kind of desperate resignation: "We're alone in dealing with this illness. Our family isn't 'normal.' How could anybody understand?"

You are not alone. Our message is simple: You are not alone. Thousands of other parents understand firsthand what you're going through. In fact, they face similar concerns every day.

In our program for children who have diabetes, we hear the same questions from parents, the same themes at the center of their lives: concerns about school, discipline, peer pressure, growth and development. Questions about getting through to angry preschoolers and withdrawn teenagers. Questions about how to balance chronic illness with everything else that matters: work, other children, and relationships.

Our experience at the International Diabetes Center, where we've worked with hundreds of children with diabetes, is backed by a variety of research, including studies at Vanderbilt University.[1] At Vanderbilt, investigators found that 70 to 80 percent of the questions heard from parents of children with diabetes and other chronic illnesses had com-

· ·

1. Nicholas Hobbs, James Perrin, et al, *Chronically Ill Children in America: Background and Recommendations.* Vanderbilt Institute for Public Policy Studies, 1983.

mon themes. In fact, most of those questions were not about managing diabetes; instead, they were about the overall job of being a parent—the same concerns all parents face.

We have also talked with our colleagues who work with children with other chronic illnesses, such as epilepsy (seizure disorder), or asthma. We discovered that these children and their parents, too, belong to the same unspoken community. Though they may be dealing with different illnesses, these people speak with a common voice; their joys, loves, and fears resonate in a common heart. And the way they join that community is through one child's illness—an illness that doesn't go away.

What we've learned is this: The parents and children in this community can learn from a common set of guidelines and principles. It's this common ground that we've tried to map in this book. On the high ground are the questions each of these parents will face: How to live each day with a child's chronic condition. How to nurture a relationship with a partner. How to work with the health care and school teams. How to relate to grandparents and the extended family.

The goal: whole parent, whole child. We know that chronic illness is a part of your life, and part of your child's life—but it is not the whole. The main point of learning how to live with a chronic illness is learning how to put this issue in perspective. When this happens, life can regain some sense of completeness. We can be whole parents of whole children.

How to Use This Book

Beyond stock answers to action. Before exploring any answers, however, we need to make one point: This book will raise a lot of questions and feelings. It asks you to think, to consider some new ideas, to do some activities. We hope you'll be active as you read—that you'll think of this book as something to experience, not a series of ready-made answers from the "experts."

There's a reason for this. We don't think anyone can give you stock answers for the questions you have about being a parent. This is true for any parent, whether or not chronic illness is part of the family picture. Besides, you know your child best.

We're communicating with each other through the pages of a book—rather than talking to each other in person. You're the expert. What you know about your child, what you see, what you feel – these are the most important things to work with. And they're things only you can know firsthand. So, don't just read this book. Use it. Think about what it says. Test what you read against your own experience. Do the activities. There's a lot of material here, but you don't have to absorb it all right now. Take one suggestion at a time and apply it to daily life. See how it works, then change your approach if that's what the situations call for.

What this book can do is help you benefit from what others have learned about raising a child with chronic illness. We can give you suggestions about what works and what doesn't. We can tell you some of the most important things we've learned at the International Diabetes Center. And, by offering practical suggestions, we can help you put new ideas into action.

One thing is certain. Children's diagnoses may be varied: diabetes, asthma, seizure disorder, or some other chronic condition. However, the issues raised for both child and parents are similar – no matter what the condition is. These people experience the same range of emotions: denial, self-doubt, exhaustion, anger, frustration, relief, joy, and love. They go through similar experiences: responding to the diagnosis, using the health care system, managing a chronic condition every day, working with teachers and school nurses, coping with emergencies, and visiting hospitals.

Get a handle on your style. In living through all of these experiences, you evolve a certain parental "style." This book is designed to help you think about your style and the needs of your child. It will help you no matter what your child's diagnosis is. What's more, children with chronic illness have the same basic emotional needs as other children, so this book can help you be a better parent for your other children as well.

Some Important Words About Our Approach

You may notice this book refers to children as either "he" or "she" rather than the generic term "they" or "he/she." You will also notice that we regularly alternate "he" and "she." We think this will make the book easier to read.

Remember, though, that when we use a specific gender, we are not making general statements about that gender. In other words, if we say "she may have a messy bedroom," we don't mean only girls have messy bedrooms.

You may also notice that this book is written as though we're speaking to parents who are married and live in a traditional nuclear family. We encourage both parents, especially parents of children with chronic illness, to be involved in their children's lives and in managing the illness. If you are a single parent or half of a divorced couple sharing custody, we wrote this book with you in mind. Yours is often the tougher task and you need all the support we can offer.

The Plan of this Book

A glance at the table of contents for this book will quickly reveal some common concerns. Each chapter focuses on an issue you're likely to face.

Chapter 1, *Entering the World of Chronic Illness*, explains the concept of chronic illness as it applies to everyone—children and adults alike. It also offers some statistics on the extent of childhood chronic illnesses in America. Besides introducing the major themes of this book, this chapter highlights some of the main issues you're likely to face soon after your child is diagnosed.

Chapter 2, *Parenthood Means Balancing Many Roles*, explores the roles you'll perform as parent of a child with a chronic illness. These roles include individual, partner, mediator, mentor, nutritionist, and child.

Chapter 3 is titled *The First Step to Success: Your Own Self-Confidence*. Here you'll find an explanation of your own self-esteem and how important it is to all parents. This chapter also offers suggestions for building your self-confidence when that's needed.

Chapter 4 is *The Crucial Factor: Your Child's Self-Confidence*. This is a companion to Chapter 3, which discusses parents' self-confidence. Chapter 4 looks specifically at how you can promote healthy self-esteem in your children.

General Points about Development is the title of Chapter 5. This part of the book highlights the landmarks in child growth and development and explains why this knowledge is important to you.

Chapter 6, *The Infant—Birth to 1 Year* expands on the discussion of growth and development in Chapter 5. Chapter 6 offers suggestions for what you can say and do to successfully meet the challenges of your child's chronic illness at this stage.

Chapter 7, *The Toddler—Your Child from 1 to 2½ Years*, discusses discipline, and provides guidelines for handling dependency, toilet-training, bedtime battles, and the like.

Chapter 8, *The Preschooler*, covers the continuing growth of the child, the child's emotional life, and your role in teaching the child self-care.

The School-Aged Child is the topic of Chapter 9. Here we provide a discussion of how personality develops during the early school years, how to build good health habits at this age, ways to widen your child's world, learning through hobbies, and fostering competence in your child.

Chapter 10 deals with *The Adolescent* and guides you as your child develops an interest in sex and sexuality and rides the emotional roller coaster of hormonal change. The challenges you confront during this time, from alcohol and AIDS to tobacco and driving are discussed.

Chapter 11, *The Everyday Concerns*, moves from theory to action. Questions that have been raised in earlier pages of the book are answered here—for children at every age.

In Chapter 12, *When You Can't Be There: Child Care Issues*, information is given about how to find, how to evaluate, and how to train babysitters and day care providers for dealing with the unique needs of your child with a chronic illness.

Chapter 13, *Working with the School Staff*, covers the relationships you must cultivate with teachers, school nurses, counselors, principals, and even school bus drivers as the parent of a child with a chronic condition. You'll learn what you have a right to expect from the educational system and what the system will expect from you and your child.

Resources: Where to Learn More is the section that lists titles of books, magazines, and other materials you may find helpful. Also included are addresses for organizations and associations which offer specific support to you as the parent of a child with a chronic illness.

What matters the most. The most important thing is this: You care enough about your child to ask, "How am I doing as a parent?" "How can I learn more?" Give yourself credit: If you're asking these questions, you must be a pretty good parent already.

Chapter One

. . . .

ENTERING THE WORLD OF CHRONIC ILLNESS

If your child has a chronic illness, remember: You are not alone. If you're sure no one can understand the emotional roller coaster ride you're on, think again: Millions of other parents are feeling the same thing right now. If you find it hard to get a handle on the anxiety, the triumphs, the tears, the joys, the mystery of it all, take heart: People across the world can echo your story.

How many people? While we don't know exactly, we can make responsible estimates. In 1985, some of the foremost authorities on this topic put the number of American children with severe chronic illness at one million.[1] These are children whose lives are circumscribed by diabetes, severe asthma, seizure disorders, leukemia, cystic fibrosis, sickle cell anemia, hemophilia, and other similar conditions. If we also include children with less severe conditions, the number jumps to 11 million—10 to 15 percent of all American children.[2]

We don't include these numbers to discourage you. If you take another viewpoint, you can even take heart in these statistics. The title of a recent book summed up this view. *We Are Not Alone: Living With*

. . . .

1. S.L. Gortmaker and W. Sappenfield, "Chronic Childhood Disorders: Prevalence and Impact," *Pediatric Clinics of North America*, Volume 31 (1984): 3–18.

2. Gortmaker and Sappenfield, 1984.

Chronic Illness.[3] If you're trying to help your child live well with chronic illness, you have plenty of company.

When you stop to think about it, it's rare for any child to be completely healthy. Almost all families have to deal with adversities and loss because there is no perfect child.

A New Reality Calls for New Action

Some people, looking at these numbers, feel we're juggling figures in a questionable way. How, they ask, can we lump together conditions such as diabetes and asthma? Cystic and leukemia?

The answer is simple: These illnesses are so much alike—not in their symptoms or diagnosis, but in the way they affect families. Nearly all these conditions have similar features. If we single out these features, we can define chronic illness accurately.

Early in this century, tuberculosis, influenza, and pneumonia were the main killers among infectious diseases. These acute illnesses could cause death in a short time if they went untreated. Fortunately, research and medication have taken them off our "most dangerous" list of fatal diseases. Most can be detected early, prevented, and cured.

In our lifetimes, acute illness, something that can be cured, has been replaced by chronic illness, something that can't be cured and won't go away, as the main health concern of Americans. Chronic illnesses are not cured, but neither do they always cause immediate death. Thus, they call for an entirely different strategy than that used for acute illness.

Other differences between acute and chronic illness are outlined below. Keep in mind that these following statements are general to many conditions; they may not apply where a specific chronic or acute illness is concerned:

. . . .

3. Sefra K. Pitzele, *We Are Not Alone: Learning to Live with Chronic Illness* (New York: Workman, 1986).

Acute illness	Chronic illness
Develops suddenly	May develop slowly—even go undetected for years
Limited in time	Usually present for a lifetime
Can often be cured	Is often controlled—not cured
Research has revealed much about the causes and course of the disease	Despite research, the causes and course of the disease are not well understood
There may be high public awareness of the disease	The general public may know little or nothing about the disease
May not call for long-term change in lifestyle	Frequently calls for radical and permanent change in lifestyle
Person with the disease is not held responsible for the disease	Personal responsibility for lifestyle (diet, exercise, quality of personal relationships) have a major effect on the condition
Often caused by an outside agent, such as bacteria or a virus	The cause may be internal: The immune system "attacks" itself or an internal organ system fails to function

Several of the differences pointed out in this table deserve more comment.

In most cases, chronic illness is forever. For the people they affect, chronic illnesses restrict choices, cause disability, and force significant changes in daily routine. And for nearly all these people, chronic illness lasts a lifetime.

It does happen that sometimes a person with chronic illness enjoys a sudden and unexplained improvement. Then we say the condition is in remission. Remission is a real possibility in several chronic conditions. Does that raise hope for being rid of the chronic illness—forever? Of course it does. For example, a child with cancer may have a remission after chemotherapy or irradiation. Everyone hopes the cancer is gone and will never come back. But sometimes it does—and the same tough treatment regimen must be tried again.

Most people with chronic health conditions live life with a day-to-day philosophy. Medical appointments, tests, medication, therapy, hospital stays—all are staples of their daily lives. And most often the routine continues for a lifetime. These people don't think of cure; instead, they talk of adjustment and learning to live new lives.

Chronic illness is mysterious and unpredictable. Faced with chronic illness, medical science is often pushed to its limits. In nearly every case, the causes are unknown. The expected outcome is uncertain. The symptoms are unpredictable. The whole course of the condition eludes our current understanding and fades into mystery.

Chronic illness strikes at the heart of who we are. Chronic illness constantly raises questions about personal identity. Self-esteem, friendship, feelings of security and independence—all these areas of life are deeply and permanently affected.

Most often, society does not blame or shame the person with the flu, diphtheria, or other acute disease. Instead, these people are seen as victims, and their presence makes others feel sympathy. Those with chronic illness, however, may feel limited as human beings—in part because the conditions last so long. In addition, most people in our society know little about cerebral palsy, cystic fibrosis, diabetes, or epilepsy. For this reason, it's hard for them to feel sympathy for those who live with these chronic illnesses. Actually, a more common response is to ignore or feel uncomfortable with the whole topic.

One parent points to this fact in speaking about his teenage son with diabetes:

Diabetes isn't something anybody else would know that Mark has by looking at him. He would have to tell others, and they would say, "Oh, well, so what?" because it doesn't show. He isn't crippled; there isn't an obvious sign. A lot of people don't think it's an immediate problem.

In short, people with chronic conditions struggle with feelings of being "different" and living outside the mainstream of society. These feelings persist, even though chronic conditions affect thousands of children.

Beyond this, the parent may seek new answers to profound questions. Even though the child may be too young to voice them, we can express some of them as:
- Who am I? If I sometimes feel I'm being held prisoner in an unresponsive body, then who is the "I" that's trapped?

- If my illness prevents me from working at the job I want or enjoying my favorite hobbies, then what do I have left?

- My friends seem uncomfortable around me. Some ignore me or avoid eye contact. How can I make them understand what I'm going through? Is something really wrong with me? Who are my true friends anyway?

- Because of my illness, my values are different. What seems so important to others doesn't matter to me. What does life really mean? How should I live?

This task of finding a new identity is complicated when people equate the person with the illness. A parent explains:

Don't say, "I'm a diabetic," or "My child is a diabetic." Say, "My child has diabetes." You don't go around saying he's a cancer, he's a pneumonia, he's an arthritis. So don't call him a diabetic. He's our son.

One final point. Chronic illness also challenges the identity of another important group in our society: the people who care for our health. Some physicians, for example, feel more competent dealing with acute illness. Why? Because professional training and medical technology equips them to handle such disease. Because cure is usually possible. And because research has yielded reliable knowledge. When dealing with acute illness, the physician can be active and in control. The patient can be more passive and is called on mainly to follow the physician's instructions. The physician knows how to "fix" things.

With chronic illness these rules may not apply. Often physicians can only monitor the illness instead of curing it. Moreover, patients often have a major responsibility in controlling the disease. In short, chronic illness forces health professionals and the people they care for into new roles—roles that none of us may be prepared for.

Chronic Illness Affects the Entire Family

One fact is certain: Chronic illness in one of your children will affect you all.

First, the child may feel many of the things we've already mentioned: a sense of isolation from other children. A feeling of being "different." A feeling of persecution—"Why did this happen to me?"—that blends into profound anger or sadness.

Beyond these, your child may face repeated medical visits to hospitals or clinics, along with the anxiety and loneliness such visits can bring. There may be pain from tests and treatments; fear of physicians or nurses who seem distant, nervous, or uncaring; fears of disability and death; boredom from languishing in waiting rooms; frustration in trying to make and keep friends.

When it hits home: reacting to the diagnosis. Parents face a whole new set of experiences, too. Many parents recall the shock when first finding out about a child's illness. They recall their desperate search for knowledge about the disease and their exhaustion from the sometimes round-the-clock care. They worry about finding good health care—and about paying for it. They often must learn a new language. They feel a loss of control. And beyond these, parents struggle with prior conflicts in their own relationships. Chronic illness in a child often forces these old tensions to the surface and makes them even more intense.

More than anything, watching a child's emotional or physical pain is a burden—pain many parents would willingly bear in the child's place. In the words of one parent, "You'd like to say, 'I'll take the disease instead.' " Though a common reaction at first, this often passes as the child matures and assumes more responsibility for self-care. The father of a boy with diabetes recalled how this fact hit home in a family conference with their health care team:

One of the things I'll always remember is when they called us together and said, "Now this isn't your disease—it's Mark's disease. Mark is the one who's going to have to learn to handle it." And that's the way it was

Soon after the diagnosis, parents commonly express a sense of isolation This surfaces in statements such as the following:

At that time we didn't know any other parents of children with chronic illnesses. At first it was all medical information coming from doctors, nurses, whatever. . . . That's one thing in the beginning we didn't get: talking to other real people.

Along with isolation may come guilt. The causes of most chronic illnesses are unclear. Even inherited diseases aren't readily understood. Right or wrong, parents hear that the disease is hereditary and they blame themselves. Even though parents know the feeling is illogical, and even though no one causes a child's chronic illness, they still wrestle with self-blame. One mother put it this way:

I guess your first reaction is, you're going to take part of the blame for it. "What did I do wrong?" But that didn't really last too long, because they made it very clear that you shouldn't blame yourself. It isn't our fault. There's nothing we could have done to prevent it.

Other emotional reactions include a general restlessness and anxiety; difficulty getting through the night; a desire to take over the child's life so the chronic illness doesn't get worse; and at the same time, a fear of dominating the child. You can hear each of those reactions in the voices of these parents:

In the very beginning, I didn't sleep much. Every time I heard a noise in the night, I thought, "Oh, David is up. Is he okay?" I don't know what you do to get rid of that anxious feeling because I think it's a natural thing you almost have to go through. You do have to work yourself out of it, though. You can't worry like that for the rest of your life. If it goes on too long, you'll need some help to get out of it.

* * *

I tried to hold back because they told me it was his disease and I was supposed to play a supportive, background role. You stay in the background, but you're still in your mind doing everything you can to check up on your child. Did he take his blood sugar reading? When? What was it? Because you think even though you're supposed to be on the outside looking in, in one way or another you feel responsible to see that he does all these things.

* * *

We cried on each other's shoulders—you're gonna do that, you know— and you accept it. I'm not saying there weren't lots of times when I cried myself to sleep. But that passed. I got over that. And I think that's a normal thing, too. That's something you have to go through.

* * *

Brothers and sisters are in this, too. And how do brothers and sisters react to the presence of chronic illness in the family? Every family responds in a unique way: still, certain problems are common. Siblings can feel neglected or passed over—second-class citizens in the family. They may feel jealousy and fear the stigma of association with a "mystery" illness.

A common charge from siblings is favoritism: Mom and Dad treat the child with a chronic illness differently; that child gets away with more and generally gets "softer" treatment. Some parents freely admit this may be true in the beginning. Still, they work hard to overcome favoritism.

I think the other kids felt—and they told me so—that I treated Mark differently and he got by with things because of the disease. And I guess I have to say my husband thinks that too. I think as time goes on you realize that this is something that's going to go on forever. We saw our son handling it as well as we could expect and realized he doesn't need to be watched all the time.

* * *

You have to treat the child with illness the same as your other children. You have to. There are times when maybe you treat him differently, but I think for his benefit as well as everybody else in the house, you have to treat these children the same or you're going to have problems. Anyway, I don't think the child with illness wants to be treated any differently.

Guilt affects siblings too. Just as parents blame themselves for chronic illness, siblings seem anxious to bear the burden of responsibility. People tell them that no one causes a chronic illness; still, siblings might not accept this at first. In the magical and irrational thinking that dominates childhood, siblings may feel somehow to blame.

The Good News: You Have a Big Impact

Robert Massie is chaplain and assistant minister at Grace Church in New York City. He has also lived with a chronic disease—severe hemophilia—since childhood. The facts of his illness include internal bleeding, arthritic pain, and damaged knee and ankle joints. His family's experiences with chronic illness are narrated by his parents in a moving book titled *Journey*.

Despite the brutal nature of this condition, Massie writes of the profound difference families can make for children. Such an illness, he says

. . . creates a tremendous need in the patient—child or adult—for a group of supportive and caring human beings who show by their words

and actions that they will stay with the patient through the physical and emotional roller-coaster ride of the disease. Thus, the single most important factor in the life of chronically ill children—other than the medical care they receive—is their relationship with their parents and family.

Children sense parental moods and attitudes and from them take the cue for their own emotional response. If the parents are fearful, despairing, or angry at the doctor (or each other), the child will feel the pressure. If the parents are supportive, patient, and caring, the child draws tremendous comfort. This is not to say that parents should be falsely cheerful or dishonest with a child, because children can almost always detect the true emotion lurking beneath a nervous smile. It is to point out what may seem a truism: that the health of any child is inextricably bound to the quality of emotional support provided by the parents.[4]

How do you make this important difference? That's what the rest of this book is about.

Look at Some Large Issues First

Before we discuss the issues that chronic illness raises for parents, and before we offer suggestions for you, we'll take the rest of this chapter to touch on some broad themes:
- Coping with change and loss
- Controlling stress
- Self-talk
- Physical and emotional contact
- Laughter
- Spirituality

Learn to cope with change and loss. "I'll have to be a full-time parent all my life." In this statement from a parent we really hear two distinct feelings: change and a sense of loss.

Perhaps the main factor in chronic illness is change. For both child and parents, life is changed forever. You must master reams of new information, adjust your schedules and daily routine, search for new means of coping, and find ways to live well with chronic illness.

....

4. Robert K. Massie, "The Constant Shadow: Reflections on the Life of a Chronically Ill Child," in Hobbs and Perrin, 1985, pp. 14–15.

Salvatore Maddi and Suzanne Kobasa, two researchers at the University of Chicago[5], have studied how people cope with change. They believe that a change in circumstances alone—such as a child developing a chronic illness—is not enough to cause psychological problems. Some people, they note, can stay healthy under great stress.

According to Maddi and Kobasa, these people share certain attitudes:
- Commitment—a sense of purpose and being actively involved in life.
- Control—a belief that they can direct the impact of stress.
- Challenge—an ability to make the best of new experiences rather than retreat from them.

You can take some steps to make these attitudes a reality in your life with chronic illness.

Get all the information you can about your child's condition. One of the most devastating aspects of change is uncertainty—not knowing what's going on, grasping for facts, feeling disoriented. This applies to any change, including the diagnosis of chronic illness in a child.

Many parents who have experienced that diagnosis have the same advice: Get educated fast. Learn all you can about your child's condition. Take classes. Read. Listen. Go to meetings. Find support groups. Ask questions, and keep asking until you understand the answers.

Comments from parents support the value of self-education:

Sometimes people are afraid to say, "Hey, I don't know this, but I want to learn this. And if I don't quite understand, I'm going to ask a question again until I understand."

* * *

After the diagnosis, our son was in the hospital for nine days, and I think we went through more schooling in that time—your head starts to swim. But it was wonderful, because we needed it.

* * *

We met with doctors, we met with nurses, we met with dietitians, psy-

....

5. Salvatore R. Maddi and Suzanne C. Kobasa, *The Hardy Executive: Health Under Stress* (Homewood, IL: Dow Jones-Irwin, 1984).

chologists, and everybody. It was a lot, but those were sessions that really helped us.

Take concrete steps to decrease your anxiety. Remember that important idea: You are not alone. And you don't have to go it alone; nobody expects that of you. There are people to turn to: your parents, other family members, friends, self-help groups, and counselors. When you do, you'll discover the truth of what we said at the beginning of this chapter: Many people are taking this journey with you.

Break change into smaller parts. When chronic illness becomes part of your life, you need to master a new set of facts and skills. Over and over again, parents confirm what a massive shock this can be. At first it overwhelms you, and you swear you'll never learn it all.

After some time passes, though, you can slowly gain perspective. After going through that stack of books and brochures for the fifth time, you understand more about your child's condition. After talking with your child's health care team, you get a sense of how you'll work together. What's more, you get a sense of what needs to be learned now and what you can worry about later.

That's the key idea. Break up big tasks into small parts. If your child has diabetes, you'll learn about insulin injections and blood testing first. All the fine details about diet, food exchanges, and insulin adjustment can be mastered more gradually, over a period of time. If your child has a seizure disorder, first learn about your child's medication, what is likely to trigger a seizure, and what action to take when a seizure occurs. Later you can read up on the medical research and find a parents' support group in your area.

Many parents find it helps to keep a journal of the most important facts they learn about their child's illness. You can also use this journal to make "to do" lists and clarify your action plan. Most of all, take it one day at a time.

Let yourself work through the feeling of loss. You may well feel loss during the first months after your child is diagnosed with a chronic illness. You mourn for your child's loss of time, potential, or choice; you also mourn for yourself.

Many parents and health care professionals offer similar advice when this happens: Don't deny your grief. Instead, allow yourself to work through that sense of loss. And don't short change or try to speed up this process.

Several writers have pointed out the stages people go through when grieving. Much of this is based on a book by Dr. Elizabeth Kubler-Ross, *On Death and Dying.*[6] Many parents feel they work through similar stages in adjusting to the fact of chronic illness. Of course, what you are adjusting to is far from death: It is life under new circumstances.

Descriptions of these stages vary, but most often you'll hear about four as first described by Kubler-Ross:

1. Denial—"This can't happen to us."
2. Anger and depression—"Why did this happen to us? We don't deserve it."
3. Bargaining—"Perhaps the doctors are wrong. If we're faithful with the medication, maybe this illness will go away."
4. Acceptance—"Chronic illness is a fact of life for our family. We'll find a way to live well in spite of it."

Two ideas emerge from this summary. First, you are apt to experience each stage, but not necessarily in this order. While not everyone goes through these stages, most people do. People also often cycle through various other feelings—not necessarily precipitated by the illness or loss. Also, the stages are not always experienced in an order as neat as perhaps is implied here. Still, don't expect to make drastic emotional leaps—for example, to go directly from denial to acceptance. People can repeat the sequence of these stages each time they experience a new loss within the chronic illness. For example, when someone with diabetes is told he has retinopathy (eye disease caused by the diabetes) he may feel the denial, anger, bargaining, and final acceptance all over again.

Parents who know about this model have told us it helps them. Why? Because it validates their feelings. It gives them some idea what to expect when first confronted with chronic illness—an experience that can be threatening and utterly new. In addition, this model gives them permission to work through their sense of loss and allow adequate time for it. Remember that the process is really more complex and personal than we can describe here, but after reading about the stages of grieving, one parent summed it up this way:

· ·

6. Elizabeth Kubler-Ross, (*On Death and Dying* New York: Macmillan, 1969).

It's good for the death and dying part, but you can put it in the same picture as chronic illness. You go through the same cycle of feelings. You have to go through it; you can't jump over it. I guess that's when you do have more problems—when you jump over the anger part or over all these things that you're going through. If you don't go through the whole process, then you're not going to be at peace about it.

One idea often helps parents move to that final stage of acceptance: the fact that acceptance is necessary, not only for the parent's health, but for the child's. In the words of one mother:

If the parents can't accept chronic illness, then the child's going to have an awful time trying to accept it.

Another parent said it this way:

I remember when I went back to work everybody said, "How come you're not a basket case?" But you've got to accept it, and you've got to make the best of it. And if I'm going to be a basket case, what help would I be to my child?

On the basis of her experience, another parent reminds us that acceptance does come. Speaking of the adjustment to chronic illness in the family, she says:

When you look back at it, there are similarities to the grieving process all the way through. It's a total process. People do go through stages where they can't accept it, or they deny it. But the end result is that you come out the other side of the whole thing with a positive attitude.

This is a good topic to learn more about. Be sure to ask your primary health care provider about it—or bring it up at a support group meeting. Chances are other parents can help you through these stages and help you reach peace and acceptance.

Learn to control stress. You know the stress response well by now: tense muscles, faster breathing, clenched fists, sweaty palms, headache, stomach in knots. Though the details of this response are different for everyone, these are common elements.

Today Americans are more aware of stress than ever before. Along with that heightened awareness has come an army of stress-control techniques. Again, you should ask your health care team about this. You can also look for resources on stress control in the last chapter of this book.

As you incorporate chronic illness into your family life, learn to recognize and control your stress reaction. Moreover, don't keep these techniques to yourself. Instead, teach your family everything you learn about this crucial subject.

When you talk to yourself, be positive. Epictetus, the ancient Roman philosopher, sounded this theme over 2000 years ago: "It's not things themselves that trouble us, but the opinions we have about these things."

He could just as well have said: We defeat ourselves by the way we talk to ourselves. This is especially true of coping with chronic illness.

When confronted with chronic illness, people start giving themselves negative messages. Some of the common thoughts that keep running through their minds are:
- "This is the worst possible thing that could happen to us."
- "I'll never make it through this."
- "Other people could handle all this, but I can't."

Think of the cumulative effect of these words. Imagine yourself locked in a room with a tape recorder that's playing these messages over and over again on an endless loop. In this situation, you could be defeated before taking any action—just through the insidious repetition of these negative statements. Think of the impact on your child.

If this mental image seems far-fetched, please reconsider: It's often not far from the truth. In moments of despair, your mind could work like that demonic tape recorder. You could well hear the same constant, negative programming.

The first step is to recognize when your mind is playing these self-defeating tapes. See if you can put your own negative self-talk into words; write it down. Then reprogram your mental computer: Turn negative statements into positive affirmations:
- "I don't like this, but we can learn to live with it."
- "I don't have to master everything right away. In time, I'll learn what I need to know."
- "Other people have learned to live well with chronic illness in the family. I'm as capable as they are. I'll learn, too. We shall overcome."

If you start to doubt the value of positive affirmation, remind yourself how powerful self-talk can be. For evidence, all you have to do is look at the power of negative self-talk to defeat you.

Ideas for positive affirmations can come from your family's own experience with chronic illness. Two examples are these:

Life with a chronic illness will give my child the reason and the energy to really take care of her health.

Living with chronic illness will help our whole family take action to eat better and feel better. We can all be healthier.

For many families, this is the real "message" of chronic illness. The title of a recent book from the International Diabetes Center drives this point home: *Learning to Live WELL With Diabetes.*[7] Diabetes is a good example, because it calls for close attention to diet, exercise, and stress control. Instead of viewing this as a burden, families can see it as an opportunity for the entire family to live well. The same could be said for other chronic conditions.

This attitude is not mere idealism. Rather, it is supported by the actual experience of families. An 18-year-old woman with diabetes confirmed this:

Having a chronic illness has disciplined other areas of my life, and it's done this for everybody in our family. We've changed our eating habits. I'm learning to live well in general, and so are Mom and Dad.

The philosopher Bertrand Russell tells of a related method for changing negative self-talk. When you fear something greatly, he writes in his book *The Conquest of Happiness*, ask yourself two questions: "What is the worst possible event that could happen in this situation?" And, "If that thing happened, what could I do in response?"[8]

This simple technique works wonders—even for children. Often our anxiety rises because we never voice our fear of the worst possible event. Simply putting this fear into words can help defuse it. This is especially true for children, though they may need your help to find the words, the pictures, or the play activities to express their fears.

. . . .

7. International Diabetes Center, *Learning to Live WELL With Diabetes* (Minneapolis, MN: 1985).

8. Bertrand Russell, *The Conquest of Happiness* (New York: Bantam, 1968).

Amazingly, we can usually think of responses to our "worst-case scenario." Doing so can boost our confidence. It can also give us ideas for positive affirmations and end the bitter cycle of negative self-talk.

Stay in contact with your family. At first this statement seems ludicrous. You may say, "Of course I'm going to stay in contact with my family. After all, we all live in the same house. We see each other every day."

Unfortunately, people lose sight of a simple fact: Simply sharing the same space does not make families intimate. How easy it is, in the crushing details of daily life, to forget to really "check in" with each other. How often do we fail to ask: "How are you feeling?" "Are you scared?" "What do you need to talk about?"

Keeping in contact means staying in touch—physically, intellectually, emotionally. We need to find out what those closest to us are thinking and feeling, including the child with chronic illness.

Beyond this we need to give and receive affection. Physical affection is an essential part of this. Sefra Pitzele, author of *We Are Not Alone: Living With Chronic Illness*, writes:

My most acute need, right now, is to be acknowledged as a person, not as a victim of chronic illness. Also, I need hugs, lots of them, and as often as possible!

When chronic illness is part of family dynamics, you need to forgive, forget, praise each other, and remind each other that you care—even more than usual. This is what we mean by staying in contact.

More insight about staying in contact comes from parents' own words:

Sometimes a man—especially if it's a boy that's sick—will have the feeling, "My son is less than perfect." They will have feelings that a lot of men don't talk about or that they wouldn't share with even their wives. They are saying to themselves, "If my son is sick, I must be less than a macho figure." That can lead to problems.

* * *

My wife and I have a real close relationship. I mean, we love each other. Our kids all see this between us. It's a loving family here, and I think that means a lot to the child with an illness.

There were times I felt neglected as a husband. She was devoting more time to our son, and it just seemed like there was no time for me. So we had to make a big effort to talk and we worked through it early on.

* * *

I think a lot of it [helping a child live well with chronic illness] is parents' support, family support. Because the kids with diabetes I know who aren't in control — their parents say, "Well whatever happens is between the child and the doctor. I don't get involved." That doesn't work. That's abandonment!

* * *

In our family, we've never done that, where you just go and shut the door, or run off when you're upset. We try to talk it out and get it out in the open. That's why our family works.

* * *

If there's a good relationship right now [between the parents just after the child's diagnosis], then they're already ahead. But if they're having any problems, whether marital or with the child, it just adds another one. You've got to work together on it; the family has to work together. You've got to be supportive.

* * *

If the parents don't care, then the child's not going to care. If the child doesn't want to help himself, then the parents can't do it. You need both.

* * *

When asked, "What's the most important advice you would give to parents who have just found out their child has a chronic illness?", one mother replied this way:

Love each other. Love the child. If your relationship with each other is shaky, you're going to have problems. If you can't talk, if a couple can't communicate with each other and say, "I hurt," or "Do you hurt?" or "What's wrong?" and talk about it . . . I know there's a lot of people who don't. They never communicate, and that's part of the problem. And then you're not going to get anywhere.

Take time to laugh. Laughter is the oldest stress-reduction technique known to our race. It's also the "healing passion," as you can see for yourself.

Notice what happens when you laugh. You smile, then your face muscles relax. That sends a rippling sensation of pleasure throughout your body. In fact, the physiological stress-reduction effects of laughing are similar to those of exercise. Both exercise and laughter may release natural "opiates." These feelings are commonly described by people who exercise, such as "runner's high."

So make time for comedy at least once each week. Cultivate sources of humor. Seek out the specific things that make you laugh.

Norman Cousins,[9] former editor of the *Saturday Review*, showed how this can be done. Cousins once suffered from collagen disease—a life-threatening illness. At one point, Cousins' chances to survive were estimated at only one in 500. To mobilize his forces for life, he used—among other things—humor. Part of his treatment regimen was a book, *The Subtreasury of American Humor*, and reruns of the television show "Candid Camera."

Cousins found that "ten minutes of genuine belly laughter had an anesthetic effect that would give me at least two hours of pain-free sleep." Certainly laughter was a key part of his eventual recovery. You can read about Cousin's triumph in his best-selling book, *Anatomy of an Illness*.

Awaken your spiritual life. Often parents find that coping with a child's chronic illness leads to a deeper spiritual life. Religion in all its forms has been concerned with issues relevant to chronic illness: overcoming suffering, coping with difficult times, learning to live with imperfection, finding a source of joy that transcends external circumstances, seeking enduring values and a purpose and meaning to life. Religious communities can create a network of caring and concerned people—people who can help your family as you learn to live well with chronic illness.

. . . .

9. Norman Cousins, *The Anatomy of an Illness: As Perceived by the Patient* (New York: W. W. Norton, 1979).

Chapter Two

· ·

PARENTHOOD MEANS BALANCING MANY ROLES .

Dreams **versus reality.** "I never thought it would be like this." Before tackling this book in detail, take some time to explore your most basic ideas and feelings about being a parent. What you envisioned parenthood to be, and what it actually is and means for you can be two very different things. In addition, you probably never expected to be a parent of a child with a chronic disease. Your feelings about these differences are real.

Remember: Even though it seems so obvious, you were once a child, too. What you know about being a parent–maybe everything you know–starts from your own childhood. From your own memories and feelings about childhood, you may have an image of the "ideal" parent. And before you became a parent, you may have daydreamed about what raising a child would be like. At the very least, you have some pretty specific ideas about what not to do.

Have your dreams matched reality? Now that you're a parent, do you catch yourself automatically talking and acting like your parents? Does this mean doing some things you swore you'd never do–such as spanking or grounding a child?

If you're surprised once in a while, you're not alone. You may also be troubled by the presence of chronic illness in your family life. Faced by this fact, you're bound to feel less confident about your abilities as a parent. In addition, it may be harder for you to discipline your child.

But, before we tackle these issues, take a minute to remember your own childhood. This will help you understand some of the things you do today as a parent. If your partner does the same, you'll understand how two people can have different perspectives on raising children.

The first step: remembering your own childhood. Take a minute to answer these questions. Have your partner do the same, then discuss your answers.

- In one word, how would you describe your parents' "style"? Were they strict? Permissive? Were they warm and affectionate? Or did they feel more distant from you?

Remember that parents can alternate between strict and permissive—or fall somewhere between these extremes. Also, their styles change over time.

- Can you think of any incidents to support your description of your parents' style? Be as specific as possible. What happened? What did your parents say and do? How did you react?
- Have you ever said, "When I become a parent, I'm going to handle this situation differently?" Or, "I'm going to handle this exactly the same way." Explain what you mean by each statement.

Learn to forgive your parents. Some people find this exercise has a surprising, but beneficial, effect. They find it easier to forgive their parents than themselves. Typical comments are these:

I still don't agree with the way my parents handled everything. But I know something now about the pressures they were under.

*   *   *

My parents were strict, kind of detached sometimes. Still, I see now that they always acted out of love for me—even if what they did sometimes seemed wrong.

*   *   *

My mom and dad were fallible. So am I. I guess there comes a time when you have to forgive them for being imperfect. That's all part of growing up.

Working, keeping a household running, paying the bills, and raising kids, too—it's all pretty overwhelming sometimes. Now that I'm doing it all, I realize what it must have been like for my parents. No wonder they made mistakes sometimes. I probably will, too.

You don't have to agree with everything your parents did before you can love them. Sure, you may decide not to spank your kids, or you may decide to show them more affection than your parents showed you, but it's important to remember: In most situations, your parents did the best they could, given the circumstances they were in.

Learn to forgive yourself for your mistakes. Remember, too, that you will do the best you can and, if you make mistakes, that's okay, too. Be able to forgive yourself and put the past behind you.

Your Many Roles

It's not accurate: People talk about being a parent as if it's one job. You know differently. Raising a child thrusts you into many new roles. So when you talk about being the best possible parent, it's logical to first look at those roles, one by one. That's the plan of this chapter.

There are many ways to approach this. For our purposes, though, we'll list seven roles:

1. Person in Your Own Right
2. Partner and Lover
3. Mediator and Parent of Other Children
4. Mentor and Guidance Counselor
5. Chef and Nutrition Manager
6. Child of Your Parents
7. Parent to your Parents

Role 1. Person in Your Own Right

Caring for yourself is not being selfish. We begin here by talking about what you're like, what you feel, what you need when you're not being a parent.

Why this approach? For two reasons:

First, there's more to life than raising children. Sure, your children are important, but if you're like most people, you have to think about a lot of other things, too. There's work: responsibilities, deadlines, office politics–all making a claim on your time and energy. There may be outside interests: church activities, volunteer work, classes you want to take. And once in a while you have to have fun, too: see a movie, visit friends, take a vacation (maybe even without the kids).

Ellen Goodman, columnist for the *Boston Globe*, says basically the same thing. She notes that her time is split three ways: personal time, professional time, and family time. If you're like her, you may feel almost like three separate persons. And each person needs special care and respect.

There's another reason for talking about your needs. Some people fall into the trap of living only for their children and through their children. Parents of a child with chronic illness are particularly vulnerable to this. Why? In part because of the demands illness makes–and the guilt, overcompensation, and self-denial that can result. These parents may think only about what their children are doing, what their children need, and what their children are feeling. If you subtracted children from the lives of these parents, there would be little–maybe nothing–left.

This is usually hard on everyone. Children often resent this, complaining that their parents are always in the way, too overprotective, always sheltering and smothering. The parents suffer, too, when children rebel or leave home to start their own families. When that happens, parents may suddenly find life meaningless and empty. The solution is to care for yourself as an individual.

Of course, there are parents at the other extreme as well–those who focus too much on themselves and their own needs. These parents need to learn how to put some focus on the child. Both types of parents need to strive for the middle ground, the ground that allows you to care for yourself and your children.

See yourself as your child sees you. As a parent, you're always observing your children, noticing how they act, what they say, seeing how they grow and change. At the same time, your children are observing you. They're making notes about what adults are supposed to be like, what children become when they grow up.

Simply by watching you, children are coming to lots of conclusions about crucial issues: what marriage is like; what working is like; what's important in life, and whether life is drudgery, joy, or something in between. That's why it's important to care for yourself as well as your children.

To drive this point home, take a minute to answer these questions:

• When during the day do you spend the most concentrated time with your child? Mealtimes? Right after supper? Weekend afternoons?

• What are you and your child doing together during those concentrated times? Eating a meal? Walking? Playing? Talking?

• Put yourself in your child's place for a moment. On the basis of watching you, what does your child learn about:
  −How to express affection?
  −How to express anger?
  −How to make friends?
  −How to spend free time?
  −How to have a good time?
  −What women should do at home and at work?
  −What men should do at home and at work?
  −What's most important in life?
  −What things are worth enjoying?
  −What things are dangerous and how to avoid them?

Write out your answers. Try to phrase them the way your child would, even if the answer startles you. For example: "The best way to make friends is to go to church and meet people." Or, "When you get angry, the best thing to do is talk very loud, leave the room, and come back later and say you're sorry."

This evaluation has two purposes. One is to see yourself for a moment through your child's eyes. The other is to realize that you're teaching your child about life all the time−simply by the example you set.

Do this with some lightness and humor; you're not trying to tear yourself down here. For right now, don't worry even if you discover something about yourself you don't like. We'll have some suggestions for change later in this book.

What do you make time for? It's one thing to sit down in a comfortable chair, when you've got time to think, and ask, "What's most important to me?" It's quite another to actually make time for the things you value the most.

The tempo of your daily life can make this painfully clear. Look at what you have to do: make a living, pay bills, referee fights between children, solve a thousand minor problems, master the details of your child's illness. Do you even have time to ask what's important?

Time: What do you make time for, and what does that say about you? For example, let's say you spend seven hours each Saturday and every Sunday afternoon on projects around the house—painting the trim, keeping the yard neat, cleaning the house. This could translate into several statements about what's important to you, such as: "My home is an investment, and I'm going to protect it." Or, "I can't stand dirt or disorder. Before I can relax, I've got to straighten things up." Or, "Puttering around the house helps me relax. This is my form of recreation, and I'm going to make time for it."

Imagine that your child had a time log that listed how you spent every hour of each day during the past week. With that evidence in hand, what would they say is most important to you? What's least important?

Step 1. You can start something like that right now. Keep a time log for two days. Choose one work day, one that represents how you usually divide your time between your job and your free time in a 24-hour period. Next, choose a "day off." This should be a day when you're primarily at home or without obligations. Then use a time log to make notes about what you do each hour on each of those days. You don't have to spend a lot of time on this. Fifteen minutes at the end of the day should do it.

At the top of these two time logs, write the word "real." These tell you how you actually spent your time on the two days you chose.

Step 2. Now take two blank time logs. Label them "ideal." Fill in these logs indicating how you would like to spend each hour of your time on a work day and a day off.

Step 3. As the final step, compare your "real" time logs with your "ideal" time logs. Keep these questions in mind:

- How closely do the logs match? Are you surprised?
- What activities are taking the most time?
- Could you make more time for an important activity?
- What activities could be eliminated without affecting the quality of your life?
- Are you actually making time for the things that matter to you most?
- If you could squeeze another free hour into the day, what would you do during that hour?
- Is there anything you want to change about the way you spend time?

Again, go easy on yourself. The purpose of this is not to give you another list of "shoulds" to be done. Rather, you're only trying to make a few discoveries about yourself.

If you do decide to change your daily schedule, take it gradually. Introduce one change at a time, using the "15-minute squeeze" technique. Let's say that you're not making any time for exercise, even though your health is important to you. Try getting up 15 minutes early for a brisk walk; go to bed 15 minutes later; or take 30 minutes for exercise during your lunch break three days each week.

Doing this can help you match your "real" time log with your "ideal" log—without trying to overhaul your life all at once.

Role 2: Partner and Lover

I'm the only one who cares. My husband just became a workaholic so he doesn't have to come home.

(Statement from a parent)

Caring for your primary adult relationship. So far we've talked about you as an individual. Now we'll move on to an equally important subject: Relationships.

By bringing up this subject, we're trying to reach parents in many different situations. Perhaps you're married, trying to share responsibility for your child equally. Many of you are single parents, doing it all alone. Maybe you're divorced, with or without custody of children from your previous marriage. Or maybe you've remarried, finding yourself with new stepchildren.

In many of these cases, parents are still concerned about a primary relationship with another adult. You might call that person a husband, wife, girlfriend, boyfriend, or "significant other," as the pop psychologists say. Here, we call that person a partner.

Perhaps there's no one in your life right now you could call a "partner." Even so, we hope you'll consider this section of the book. Why? Because raising a child with a chronic illness will enter into any relationship that is part of your life.

Here we have to raise another question: Where do we get our ideas about what relationships should be like? Today we get lots of suggestions, but many of them may not work for us.

If you grew up in the 1950s, some of your ideas about family life have probably come from television. Shows such as "Leave It To Beaver" and "Father Knows Best" presented us with the traditional family: Mother at home full-time, Father at work full-time (even though no one ever quite understood just what Father did). Dad was usually in a suit and tie, even when he was at home. He ran the family like an efficient business. Mom was freshly made up, always cheerful, impeccably dressed, always available to her children. The children got into trouble, but none of the family problems were really that serious. Mom and Dad never seemed to have any personal problems. And, if the going got tough, you could count on both parents being there to see it through.

Today, our images of the family have changed. Now television presents us with single-parent families, divorce, step-families, adoption, and even affairs. But, sometimes television, as well as magazines, newspapers, and movies, still tells us it's possible to find the perfect relationship. And none of them say much about what it's like to raise a child with a chronic illness and still hold onto that perfect relationship.

Reflect on your relationship. It's time again to discover something about yourself—this time about the primary adult in your life. We could ask all kinds of vague questions, such as, "What is your marriage like?" "Is your relationship working?" "Are you fulfilled?" But instead, we'll get a little more down-to-earth.

Answer the following questions, and ask your partner to answer them, too. Don't do this together, however. You should write out your own answers.

• When am I with my partner during a typical day? While getting up and getting ready for the day? During breakfast, lunch, or dinner? During the early or late evening?

• What do we do during the times just listed? Are we giving primary attention to each other? Or, are we doing several things at the same time – eating, talking to children, washing the dishes, running errands, or talking about the child's medical regime?

• When do we spend concentrated time with each other – away from the children, TV, meetings, housework, jobs, and other outside activities? What do we do during those times? What do we talk about?

• Does my partner know what worries me currently? What excites me and gives me hope? Could my partner accurately explain what I do for a living?

• Do we talk about more than the routine problems of daily life? Could my partner explain what's most important to me, what I'd like to be doing in five years? Could my partner sum up my basic stands on politics and religion?

• Imagine that your partner could take a fully paid sabbatical from work, spending the time in any way he or she pleases. Can you predict what your partner would do during that year?

• Do we talk openly about our child's chronic illness? Is this a subject we bring up often? How do I feel when this topic comes up? How does my partner feel? What is the tone of this conversation – frightened, accusing, sad, excitable?

• Do we express affection for each other? How? When?

Now share what you've written with your partner. You may go over this material together; you can also choose a separate time to go over your partner's answers alone. In either case, don't judge the answers right away. Try to understand your partner's viewpoint first.

These questions and answers can tell you about three key things:

1. How well you know each other – and how well you thought you knew each other.

2. How you spend your time together—what you talk about and what you do.

3. How you demonstrate your feelings to each other.

We're not trying to analyze your relationship here or put you through marriage counseling. (You may decide these on your own.) Still, you might decide to work on some part of your relationship after answering these questions. If you do, pick a limited goal and chose one thing you can do right away to move toward that goal.

Let's say your goal is to spend more time alone, without your children. Ask yourselves what prevents you from doing that right now. Is it that you don't have a dependable sitter? Then make it your goal during the next month to find one. Ask everyone you know—neighbors, friends, people at work, health care providers, day-care centers—to recommend someone. When you've found a sitter you can trust, then set a "date" to go out with your partner. Stick to that date, reminding yourself that it's the most important thing on your calendar for the next month.

Role 3: Mediator

Richard was my little brother. He was valiant in my defense, standing in front of me and proclaiming: "You let my sister be!" But he was also frail, and his frequent illnesses reinforced my father's overprotectiveness toward his only son. I have a few memories of genuine battles— there was a doll he smashed and the broken latch of my door at the farm, which he battered with a hammer, and once I was spanked because I had hit him. But, in general, our life together was placid and unexciting. Most of the pranks we played were my inventions, and whenever he tried to conceal any of our misdeeds, he would blush scarlet under his fair skin, for he was embarrassingly truthful.

Blackberry Winter, Margaret Mead

You're raising a child with a chronic illness and that consumes a lot of your time and energy. For, not only is your child coping with a chronic illness—so are you.

But, what if you have other children? Do they get along with each other? Are they competing for your time and attention? Do they feel the child with chronic illness gets too much attention? Are you setting different limits for that child and giving him more attention? You may not feel you are, but what do the other children think?

All these questions point to another role thrust upon you: Mediator. As mediator, your job is to defuse the tensions between your children.

Why do brothers and sisters get along sometimes – and why don't they at others? There are lots of issues to consider, even for families who are not coping with illness. Some of the factors that affect how your children get along with each other include:

• **The spread in the children's ages.** For example, take the couple with two children born one year apart. At one point, both of these children were in diapers. Both were going through similar stages. Both were making the same kinds of demands on the parents. This is a situation that might build competition from the start.

• **Things you do and say – without knowing it – that make children feel they have to compete for your affection.** Do you ever refer to one child as your "favorite" daughter or son, either by words or, more likely, by actions? If one child shares an interest of yours, do you dwell on that child's achievements?

• **Comparisons.** These can be far more subtle than saying, "Why can't you be more like your brother?" Assigning different labels to your children: "He's the athlete," "She's the musician," "He's the smart kid in school," "She's the perfectionist" – all can be forms of comparison, too.

In his book, *The Strong-Willed Child,* James Dobson discusses jealousy between children. He advises that the first step is to avoid circumstances which compare children unfavorably with each other. Parents should guard against comparative statements about their children particularly in these areas: physical appearance, intelligence, and athletic ability. Children are extremely sensitive about these areas because so much of their self-esteem depends on how they are viewed here. In short, in matters relative to beauty, brains, and athletic prowess, each child should know that in his parents' eyes, he is respected and has equal worth with his siblings.

• **The order of your children's births.** Your first child had all your time and attention for a while. That may make a real difference in the kind of environment you provided for that child. Some studies say that firstborns may get more intellectual and emotional stimulation.

Other studies say that later-born children face unique problems. These children may feel they're always compared to the older brother or sister. For that reason, later children may have a harder time establishing their own identities.

These things may apply to your children—or they may not. Remember that psychologists make general statements about groups of children; their theories may not hold true for your child.

Yet, birth order is worth some thought. Think about your family. Do you see any differences in your children that might be accounted for by birth order? Do some conflicts between your children stem mainly from this factor? Later we offer some suggestions for helping your children get along, but for now, our purpose is to raise this issue and encourage you to think about it.

Why have more than one child? For some people today, only one question in life looms larger than "Should we have children?" That bigger question is: "Should we have more than one child?" "Should we consider adoption?" "Should we give our child a brother or sister?"

Please note: We understand that these questions do not apply to all of you reading this book. Perhaps you've already decided not to have more children. Perhaps another child is not even an option for you. While acknowledging these facts, we still want to speak to this issue.

Earlier we talked about rivalry between brothers and sisters. Certainly there's one way to avoid that problem: Have only one child! But is that the best solution? Not necessarily!

There are some real arguments for providing your child with a brother or sister. Every family situation is different, and no one can say that you must have more than one child. But consider some possible factors in your decision.

In families with more than one child, a child learns firsthand what it's like to function in a close group. This group—your family—is different than any other group she'll find herself in. Schoolmates, Cub Scouts, Girl Scouts—none of these offer the same tensions or the same opportunities for warmth. Getting along with a sibling is an experience your child will find nowhere else.

What's to be gained from that experience? The support that only a brother or sister can give. When your children are screaming at each other, this truth will seem far removed from reality. In time, though, it will become clear how important these sibling ties are. More specifically, siblings can give you another perspective on your family–the primary source of your self-esteem.

Self-esteem (or self-confidence) is probably the main driving force in all of us. Where we live, who we marry, where we work, how well we feel–all these choices rest on this primary decision. We make a basic decision about self-esteem early in life, though we can change it based on later life experiences. (More on this in Chapters 3 and 4.)

Our first and most important cues for making this decision come from the family–especially from the relationship with our parents. Our perspective on that first relationship changes as we get older. For example, you may feel that your older brother or sister got more opportunities in childhood than you did. This was the brother who excelled in school, in sports, in music. Perhaps you feel your parents spent more time with this sibling, or paid more for his music lessons, or spent more time helping her with homework.

For some people this results not only in resentments, but in lower self-esteem: I didn't get attention because my parents didn't like me as much. Therefore, I wasn't worthy.

A brother or sister can help you work through this. Your brother can explain the self-doubts and fears he had–feelings you weren't aware of Your sister can help dispel your conflict about favoritism in the family. In short, a sibling can give you another chapter in your family's story, a chapter that can add to and clarify your own understanding.

Also, consider some other reasons for providing siblings:

• **Your children will learn new things**–ideas that spring from an older sibling's experience, things that an adult forgets.

• **Your children learn how to make their way in a group of other children**–peers, more or less. There's practical experience in working things out, in resolving conflict, in considering other children's feelings. And all this occurs in an environment you closely monitor: your home

• **A sibling may offer support for living with chronic illness**– support that you or the ill child simply cannot provide. A sibling, being still a child, is, in some deep and unspoken way, a powerful ally for the brother or sister with chronic illness. The emotional support and concern from this ally has an impact that no adult can have.

Role 4: Mentor and Guidance Counselor

The question of discipline was important to all the parents. Setting limits was described as teaching children various forms of control as well as acceptable behavior. Several parents acknowledged that disciplining their diabetic youngsters was more difficult than setting limits for their non-diabetic children. Feeling sad about the pressures already put on their diabetic youngsters, parents did not want to "inflict" an additional burden on them.

After much discussion, the group members came to look on this as a disservice to their children. In the long run, they would not learn acceptable behavior and would, as a consequence, be less well prepared for the future.

One mother, when she recognized that her own "buried pain" was causing her to treat her son differently from his brothers and sisters, realized that "he doesn't really want to be special, and it's harmful to him to be treated that way."

> Joan B. Leibovich, "Parents of Diabetic Youngsters
> Look at Themselves," *Diabetes Forecast*, May/June, 1977.

So far we've discussed only three of the "hats" you must wear as a parent: individual, partner, and mediator. Yet you have to play other roles, too. Among the most important is mentor.

Before we attack the questions, we need to define "mentor." By this word, we mean all the duties normally included by the words "discipline" and "setting limits." We prefer the term mentor, however, because it gets at the root meaning of all these terms. When you act as a mentor, you're a counselor, a guide, a teacher, and a coach.

Isn't this the real meaning of disciplining a child? After all, other teachers and coaches instruct your child in a certain subject—say, English, math, or football. But you are your child's mentor for life as a whole. When you set limits or punish a child, you're teaching basic values that will guide that child in all avenues of life. In short, while other mentors help your child succeed in a certain subject, you help your child to succeed as a person.

There's another way to approach this idea. The word "discipline" is much like "disciple," and that similarity can help us. We don't mean to imply anything religious here. What we do say is this: The relationship between parent and child is like the relationship between master and disciple.

In other times, the master was someone who excelled in a certain branch of knowledge or art: the disciple was the follower, a person molded and influenced by the master. In this sense, your child is your disciple—at least for a while. What you're teaching, however, is not a particular art or craft, but the art of living.

Being a mentor means constantly influencing your child's behavior. How do you do this? In many ways. For example:

- Scolding
- Spanking
- Using "time-outs" or isolating your child in a bedroom
- Praising
- Blaming
- Reasoning
- Altering the tone of your voice
- Changing your body language—the tension or relaxation in your facial expression; the posture you adopt when talking to your child.

If you have been a parent for some time now, you've developed a parental "style" of your own. When we talk about style, we refer to the ways you use—or avoid—actions such as those listed above.

What's your style as mentor? Take some time now to think about your style as mentor. Try to answer these questions:

- What do I say to my children when I've had a rotten day at work and I just want to be alone for a while?

- What do I do when my child fusses uncontrollably or screams in a restaurant or store?

- What do I tell my children about keeping their rooms clean? How do I react when my child's bedroom looks like a construction site?

- How do I explain chronic illness to my children? Do I speak strictly in factual terms? Do I use stories about other children with a similar condition? What do I feel when the topic comes up? Do I become more tense physically; does my tone of voice change?

- How much time do I spend giving my child full, undivided attention—away from the TV, newspaper, and my other projects? Do I give the same amount of this quality time to each of my children?

- Could I sum up in a few simple sentences my approach to raising children? Could I list the most important values I'd like to pass on to my children?

- Do I set limits? Do each of my children know the limits I've set for their behavior? When did I last discuss these limits with them?

- What do I do at the breakfast table? Do I read the paper? Do I make conversation with my family? Do I ask about my child's day?

- How do I react when my teenager is playing the stereo at ear-shattering volume? What do I say to that child? What punishment—if any—do I impose?

We offer some specific guidelines for discipline later in this book—that is, for being an effective mentor. For now, however, our purpose is to get you thinking about the kind of mentor you are today, and the kind of mentor you want to be.

Role 5: Chef and Nutrition Manager

All parents have to make decisions that directly affect their children's health. As the parent of a child with a chronic illness, the decisions you make about nutrition are even more crucial: The way your child eats could be a major factor in controlling the illness. This involves you in another role: nutrition manager.

Again, we'll offer some specific guidelines for nutrition later, but here we'd like you to think about the way you're currently handling the nutrition manager role.

Look at the way you're eating now. For many people with chronic illness, reality hits home three times a day at the kitchen table. Chances are good you'll need to change your child's diet for medical reasons—which may mean changing your own diet, too. This leads to a new thought, one that may trigger some fear and even anxiety: "We can't eat the way we used to."

In many cases, you simply have to change. Eating well is crucial to managing many chronic conditions, such as diabetes. So, you may have to give the act of eating much more attention than you're used to. This might be hard. You may even resent it.

After all, food can be a security blanket of sorts, a crutch for relaxing and staving off anxiety. When things are going badly at work, do you mentally savor your favorite dessert? In the middle of tense or draining meetings, do you daydream about the martini or the beer that's going to help you relax and shake off the day? Do you crave a slice of chocolate cheesecake to reward yourself?

Can you find ways to handle stress without using food or alcohol?

Something else makes changing your diet hard: knowing where to start. Rather than plunging in and making an arbitrary choice–"We're going to cut out ice cream and cake," or "From now on, it's only granola at breakfast"–do something else first. Start by understanding what you're doing with food right now.

This is only common sense: Before you can fix anything, you've got to know what's broken. How do you find out what's working and what's not with the way you eat today? Keep a food diary.

For now, you don't have to change anything. Just keep notes for one week about when and what you eat. Again, this doesn't have to take a lot of time; you can probably write up the day's entry in 10 to 15 minutes.

What do you write about? Just jot down answers to these questions:

• When did we eat today?

• Which meals did we eat at home as a family? Which did we eat at school or work?

• What's the biggest meal of the day? The lightest meal?

• When we eat at home, who plans and prepares meals? Is this a shared task, or does one person have the main responsibility?

• Did we eat in a relaxed manner, taking time to talk and share the news of the day? Or did we "graze," with family members eating on the run between commitments?

- What did we eat at each meal? (If you don't know the menu for every-one's meals, just write down the basic food groups represented in the meal: fruits, vegetables, meats, dairy products, breads and grains.)

- Did you or your children snack during the day? If so, when and what was eaten?

- Do you eat to celebrate or to relieve stress? At what specific times? What kinds of food do you eat?

- Do you reward your family with food?

Involve the whole family—and don't point fingers. Ask your children and partner for help with this task. Explain the reason for keeping a food diary: To look for broad patterns in the way your family eats, and to look for the best point to start changing your diet. Let them know, too, that no one is trying to assess blame or point a finger. At this point, you're like a scientist doing research and trying to be neutral and objective. Later, we'll talk about using this information and actually changing your diet.

Role 6: Child of Your Parents

This role is easy to overlook, but it's one that colors almost every decision you make as a parent. This role is based on one fact: You are a child, too. Your parents—your children's grandparents—will be a decisive factor in your children's lives. It's a new phase for grandparents, too. Having a child thrusts you into a new stage of life, just as coping with chronic illness does. It's easy to forget that other people with a stake in your child's life are also entering a new stage. These people are grandparents.

Becoming a parent means, first of all, seeing your parents with new eyes and feeling new emotions toward them. Some examples come from the following statements by new parents:

I finally understand what Mom and Dad were going through in trying to raise kids. This is hard work!

* * *

My parents sure weren't perfect. But I've learned something: You make mistakes sometimes just because you're tired or you honestly don't know what to do.

* * *

My husband helps take care of the baby, but Mom did it all alone. With three of us to worry about, it must have been just too much sometimes.

At the same time, your parents are faced with new realities:

- Being "old enough" to be grandparents.

- Realizing that their children are really grown up. The chance to directly influence and mold children may be gone. The job of parenting may be done. In short, they have to let go.

- Wanting to be useful, to show that their lives are worthwhile; wanting to confirm that they have advice to give and wisdom to share.

- Wishing to make things easier for you, to help in any way possible. This feeling may be especially intense when you have a child with chronic illness.

- Wanting to be closer to you, talk to you more, stay in closer touch. This could mean new demands—including higher long-distance phone bills, constant reminders about getting current family pictures, and frequent requests to visit.

Of course your parents probably feel only some of these things—and there are many variations. The main point, however, is this: With the birth of your child, their lives are changing, too.

What's your style with grandparents? You're a new person, and so are your parents. Now you have a new relationship to sort out, a new balance to achieve. You can expect this to take some time—and perhaps you should expect a few hassles, too.

One problem is common with grandparents when a child with chronic illness is involved: favoritism. It's easy for grandparents to smother this child with "goodies"—extra food, toys, clothes, attention, and time. Much of this behavior may be fueled by pity and sorrow—something that's painfully obvious to you and your child. What's more, other grandchildren may feel excluded.

How would you respond to this situation? Read these sample responses and see if one of them matches your style:

Why are you doing this? You're just spoiling her. This shower of good-ies has just got to stop.

* * *

We're worried that she might use her epilepsy to get attention. Also, we don't want her to feel so strongly that she's "different," and we don't want her to feel sorry for herself.

* * *

Thanks so much for all you're doing. You're the best grandparents he could have.

* * *

It's obvious you love your granddaughter, and we really appreciate the things you do. But, maybe it's time to ease off for a little while.

We'll offer suggestions for improving your relationship with grandpar-ents in following chapters. For now, just think about the above state-ments. Are any too aggressive for you? Too easy on the grandparents? Do any do justice to both your own feelings and grandparents' feelings? Choose one of these statements (or invent one of your own), and then explain why you'd use it.

Remember: Grandparents choose their style, too. As a parent, you have your own style. That style is the sum of all the choices you make, the way you solve problems, the things you say and do when you're with children.

It's easy to forget, though, that grandparents have their own style. They can be close friends, knowing the details of your children's lives almost as well as you do. Or, they can be removed from daily events, yet reliable and affectionate when you need them. At times, they can be distant, even cautious. Again, there can be great variations in their actions and reactions.

Too many misunderstandings between parents and grandparents have their root in one source: different ideas about what grandparents are supposed to be. It's easy for you to assume one role for grandparents while they're assuming an entirely different one.

The way to defuse this potential conflict is to get your feelings out in the open. You may be expecting certain things from grandparents without realizing it. When you're not aware of those expectations, then grandparents usually aren't either.

What do you want grandparents to be? When do you expect them to "be there" for your children? Think about what you'd like grandparents to say and do when:

- You first find out your child has a chronic illness.
- Your child has her first birthday.
- You're exhausted, tired of constantly solving problems, and wanting a break.
- Your child has to enter the hospital.
- You're set to go out to dinner and a movie and your babysitter cancels at the last minute. Your only choice is to call grandparents.
- Paying for your child's medical care is becoming tough, and you're short on money for the rest of the month.
- You're going overseas for a vacation, and you'd like someone to take the children for two weeks.
- You need help with house projects—spring cleaning, fixing the garage, building a playhouse—and you're too exhausted to tackle any of it.

From these thoughts may come some questions for grandparents: How often would you be willing to babysit? How often would you like to visit? If we need financial help, could we come to you?

And, if you have questions, why not ask them now? You don't have to spring them all at once in a marathon session. But, do put one or two questions foremost in your mind and ask them when the time is right.

Anticipate how to handle specific situations. What happens when you feel that grandparents are spoiling your child? Use this scenario as one example of thinking ahead, of choosing your style before the situation actually occurs. Say that grandparents are showering the child with toys, clothes, extra holiday gifts, or a generous allowance. They feel sorry for your child and you don't like any of it. How would you handle the situation?

After thinking about this for a while, consider these possible responses. Think about their merits and weaknesses:

I can see how much you love Melissa. And we really appreciate the attention you give her. But we'd prefer that you not give her extra gifts and goodies. We don't want her to think that illness is the best way to win affection and attention. Maybe we can find some other ways you can help that would help her feel more capable and successful.

* * *

All that stuff is just cluttering the house. Are you crazy? You're just spoiling him.

* * *

Thanks so much. You're just too kind—the best grandparent in the world.

Role 7: The "Parent" of Your Parents

Many of us will face yet another role in our lifetimes—when we must take over responsibility for much of the care of our own parents. When you are caring for a child with a chronic illness and for a parent who is debilitated or also chronically ill, the support of your own parents as we have presented it is not available to you.

Today many couples are marrying later and choosing to delay starting a family. This means older and not necessarily healthier grandparents. Although these parents (grandparents) are living well into their 80s, our relationships with them must change. One late-middle-aged mom wrote:

How I wish we could die healthy! My husband and I had a bit of an afterthought. As I readjusted to diapers again after just getting my youngest off to kindergarten, my mom fell and broke her hip. It's been down hill ever since as I'm torn between infant and parent with their needs so similar. I've tried to search out community resources for help, but even that takes time and energy I don't seem to have.

If you come from a family that values, even insists, that grandparents are taken care of at home, and you have a chronically ill child to care for, the pressure can be intense, both internal and external.

Services for the elderly are more available, but our mobile society results in families being spread all over the globe. Care of an ailing parent and decisions about that care or use of various services must often be facilitated long-distance or perhaps loaded onto the one adult child living in closest proximity. If there's a chronically ill child in that equation, the care must be shared and community "helps" used to their fullest potential.

Look under Home Care Services in the Yellow Pages of the phone book. Call the most well-established nursing home in your area and ask about programs in your community to care for elderly disabled people at home.

Get counseling support for yourself as the responsible caretaker to make certain you're coping and caring for yourself adequately. People and programs want to help. Some are better organized and publicized than others. Search out the right help.

Chapter Three

· ·

THE FIRST STEP: YOUR OWN SELF-CONFIDENCE

What allows you to take on all the parental roles we talked about in Chapter 2? For one, it takes physical energy. That's often scarce when you're up four times in the night because of an ear infection, or when you end up bringing work home and not starting it until 9:30 when the kids are finally in bed.

Then there's another kind of energy – a mental and emotional energy. We call it self-esteem or self-confidence. In this chapter, we'll talk about your self-confidence: what it is, how to boost it when it's low, and how self-confidence begins with our expectations.

Why You Should Care for Yourself

Perhaps you're a little suspicious of all this talk about self-esteem. Bookstore shelves are jammed with self-help titles. Leo Buscaglia is on television hugging people and practically shouting at you to feel wonderful about yourself. When you're feeling low, friends say, "You've just got to like yourself more."

All of this is so easy to say. Self-respect, self-love, self-esteem – isn't it all just a little self-centered? Does it really mean anything? And how does it apply to raising children?

We can't blame you for feeling this way. In this chapter, we'll try to think clearly about self-confidence and how it matters to you.

Think of self-confidence not as feelings but as energy for action. When that energy is high, you can say:

We made it through a serious seizure. Next time I won't be so frightened because I know I can manage.

* * *

I really had needle phobia, but my child's life depends on this. I did it. Tomorrow I'll be able to do it again.

* * *

Asthma really scares me. The thought that my child might stop breathing shakes me up when I think about it. But I will be able to do what's needed.

Each of these statements is realistic. They don't gloss over suffering and struggle with a pat phrase. And yet they convey a common feeling: It's tough, but we're up to the job when it really counts.

If you've understood this, then you can also predict the results of low self-confidence. When you're low on this vital energy, you feel like you're on a permanent downward spiral. Chronic illness seems too much to handle, and you're not on top of it. If you're thinking this way for weeks or months at a time, you may be dangerously low on self-confidence.

Your child sees all this, too. If you're confident, then your child can say, "Things really are okay. Mom and dad aren't worried all the time, so I don't have to worry either." On the other hand, your low self-confidence can sink your child's hopes and make him feel like a burden. This underlines an important fact: When you work on your own self-confidence, you're also helping your child.

Boosting Your Self-Confidence When It's Low

There were allergies on my side of the family. I'm sure that's why Johnny got asthma. My husband Bill blames me, too.

I saw Charlie shaking and I just knew he was putting it on, and I was really mad. But then I found out that it wasn't an act. I felt so awful. I just guess I'm a lousy father.

You may agree that self-confidence is essential. Simply saying this, however, is usually not enough. When you feel you've made serious mistakes with your child's illness, or when you anticipate failure in the future, you need something more.

To build your self-confidence, work on three fronts: **Knowledge, feelings, and action.**

Increase your knowledge. One of the devastating things about dealing with chronic illness is uncertainty. You simply don't know what's going on with your child's body. It's all a mystery to you.

So, get informed. Ask your health care provider questions and keep asking until you understand. Read. Write to organizations for literature on your child's condition. (See the list at the end of the book in the section called "Resources.") And when you don't understand something, admit it. It's okay. It's far worse for both you and your child if you cover up ignorance.

Bring your feelings to light. It's hard to admit that you're not feeling equal to the task of raising your child. Remember, however, that there are two basic ways to deal with anxiety: You can try to escape **from** it, or you can escape **into** it.

Escaping from fear usually leads to self-defeating behavior: long stretches in front of the television set, a couple more drinks after dinner, withdrawing from your family, increased overtime at work. None of these really work for reasons captured in the current lament: "You can run, but you can't hide."

Escaping **into** fear, odd as it may sound, offers more hope. This means bringing your self-doubt, fear, and anxiety out into the open. At the beginning, this may feel like putting the messiest closet in your house on public display, but there is something you can do about it.

Help yourself, first of all, by learning to relax. Why? Because relaxation will calm you when you bring negative feelings to the surface. When you're relaxed, you won't be tempted to run and hide, and you'll sidestep defeat.

What we've learned about the human body in recent years suggests that relaxation is something you learn. Don't assume that you know how to relax already, or that you relax when you sleep. Actually relaxation is a skill, and with practice you can get better at it. When you do get better, you can call on this "relaxation response" any time during the day. To learn more about relaxation, look in the Resources section at the end of the book.

At the same time that you're learning to relax, seek out other people. You don't have to go it alone. Lots of other people have raised children with chronic illnesses. And, as we pointed out in Chapter 1, many are doing it now, today.

Remember a basic premise of this book: One child may have epilepsy, another asthma, diabetes, or another chronic condition, yet the struggles and self-doubts faced by their parents are much the same, regardless of the diagnosis. All these people have to get the best possible medical care and pay for it; all have to live with the condition 24 hours a day; all have to balance being a parent with other roles in life. Find some of these people and talk with them.

Talking could mean joining a local support group. Or it may mean getting to know one other family that copes well. Either option is fine. The most important thing is to learn firsthand that you are not alone. When you do, your self-confidence will stabilize and grow.

Learn how to act for change and take action. Another way to boost your self-confidence is to see positive change occur in your life. Even a small change can start the ball rolling. So start with a small change. You can't make yourself over in one day, so why try? Besides, being overly ambitious can lead to wasted effort and a feeling of failure.

Try just two things: Choose an overall goal relating to your child's illness, and then decide on one specific action you can take to realize that goal. For example:
- "I want to know more."
- "I want to be well prepared for an emergency (such as an insulin reaction, a seizure, or an asthma episode.)"
- "I want to meet other people who are raising a child with similar problems."

Choose one goal—just one. Plan to focus on it for the next month. Then, decide on the action you can take. Make the action small enough and definite enough to try right away, but don't do busywork. Make sure the action implies a meaningful step to your goal. For example:

- **Goal:** To know more about my child's illness.

   Action: I'll keep a pad and pencil handy so I can jot down questions as they occur to me. Then I'll bring that pad with me and ask those questions at our next doctor's appointment.

- **Goal:** To be well prepared for an emergency.

   Action: I'll find out where I can take a class in CPR (cardiopulmonary resuscitation). Then I'll sign up and make the time to go.

- **Goal:** To meet other people with chronically ill children.

   Action: I'll find addresses for national diabetes, asthma, or epilepsy groups. Then I'll write, asking if there are support groups in my city.

The Family Inside Your Head—and the Script It Writes

In the late 1960s, several best-selling books touted a new way of talking about psychotherapy. Among them were *Games People Play* by Eric Berne, M.D.,[1] and *I'm OK—You're OK* by Thomas Harris, M.D.[2] Both men called their methods "transactional analysis," a term that need not be defined here.

Several useful ideas did emerge from this popular movement in psychology, however. One was the idea that our personalities really consist of three "voices," three sets of feelings and ideas. These voices are talking to each other in a kind of permanent conversation, and they say a lot. Among the things these voices decide are how we'll act in any situation and (our main concern here) how good or bad we are.

The Parent, Adult, and Child. One voice Harris called the "Parent"— memories of everything our biological parents said and did. In the "Parent" is lodged the advice, warnings, and wisdom of our real parents, such as:

- Cleanliness is next to godliness.
- When you're behind, don't give up, no matter what.
- It's not womanly to be vice-president of a corporation.

. . . .

1. Eric Berne, *Games People Play* (New York: Grove Press, 1964).

2. Thomas Harris, *I'm OK—You're OK: A Practical Guide to Transactional Analysis* (New York: Harper & Row, 1967).

When you grow up, you may dispute these ideas; some you'll even reject. However, other ideas you've never questioned are still there in the "Parent," helping to determine how you act today.

Another voice in us is the "Child." The "Child" is like a recording of our responses to events—mainly feelings about our parents, our brothers and sisters, and the events of daily life. Many of these "recordings" date back to our first five years of life. This is a time of helplessness, a time when we depend on our parents for everything. As young children, we want to win the affection of our parents. When we don't gain that affection, or when something happens that we don't understand, the "Child" in us often assumes the worst:

- When something goes wrong, it's always my fault.
- My mom (or my friend) got mad at me today, so I'm a bad person.
- I want everyone to like me, and if they don't, it's terrible.

However, many of the "Child's" feelings are good and useful all our lives. Among those useful feelings are a sense of wonder, a delight in games and play, joy, and laughter.

The third voice in our personality is the "Adult," a voice that actually starts around our first birthday, when we learn to walk. Walking is important because it marks the first time we explore the world independently. This is literally the first step to becoming an individual. Now we can explore the world beyond our mother's breast and father's lap.

As we grow older, we continue to explore. We think; we reflect on our experience. We test the admonitions of the "Parent" and the feelings of the "Child" to see if they ring true with our own experience. In a healthy personality, the "Adult" sifts through the tape recordings made by the "Child" and the "Parent." The "Adult" decides which messages are true and useful and saves those; the questionable ideas and feelings are filed for further testing. The useless and untrue recordings are erased.

What script are you acting out right now? Among other things, these three voices produce a script for your life. For a play or TV show, the script includes directions that tell the actors how to move, what to say, and how they should react to events. Likewise, our internal script is a set of directions for the character we play in life. The scripts can be long and complicated, but some of their main ideas can be summarized in a few sentences.

Everyone's script is different, but some typical directions might be these:

When there's conflict between people, it's my job to make peace.

* * *

I can only feel okay if I win everyone's approval.

* * *

The most important thing is that people be nice to each other. If people disagree, do something to cover it up at all costs.

* * *

It's not okay to show anger—or even to feel it.

By playing with this idea of scripts, you might gain some insight into yourself. What's useful right now is to think about your parental script. This is the whole set of ideas you inherited about how to raise children. Who wrote that script? Parent, Child, or Adult? Have you ever dusted off that script and taken a look at it with a critical eye?

Did you choose the script you're playing now? Your parental script might benefit from a little editing—underscoring the good parts, crossing out the bad parts, rewriting some crucial lines. The following exercise will help you start.

Brainstorm for five minutes on these three questions. This is a kind of "fill in the blank" exercise—only there are no "wrong" answers. And, you should think of as many answers as you can. The questions are short:

1. Fathers are supposed to be . . .
2. Mothers are supposed to be . . .
3. Parents should cope with a child's chronic illness by . . .

One thing is important: Don't censor or judge any of your answers. Write them down as quickly as you think of them, and don't worry about how they sound.

Here are some answers other people have supplied:
- Mothers are supposed to—
  —Stay home when your child is too sick to go anywhere.

—Not be seen drinking.
—Keep the peace and always be cheerful.
—Be gentle all the time.
—Be strong all the time.
—Plan meals and buy groceries.
—Clean, do laundry, and wash dishes.
—Quit work if a child demands full-time care.

• Fathers are supposed to—
—Make money.
—Make the most money.
—Work hard.
—Handle the worst discipline problems.
—Talk to the mechanic when the car goes in for repair.
—Be the bulwark of the family and never "crack."
—Do most of the driving on family vacations.
—Enforce the rules of the household.

• Parents should cope with a child's chronic illness by—
—Always being calm and in control.
—Never questioning the child's physician.
—Working twice as hard as other parents to make sure the child gets a decent chance in life.
—Understanding all the medical details about the child's condition.
—Making their children the most important part of their lives.

Your list of invisible "shoulds" is probably longest when it relates to the third question—to chronic illness. Here are some other actual responses from parents:

• *I should always manage the care routine—such as testing, deciding what activities are okay, giving shots, and planning food.*

* * *

• *When my child is away from home, I should worry about how she's doing. In fact, I should check on her frequently*

* * *

- *I need to manage all the meals for everyone in the family.*

* * *

- *When my child has a seizure (or an insulin reaction, or an asthma episode), I should always be calm and in charge.*

* * *

- *When I talk to friends and family about my child's illness, I should also appear calm and competent.*

* * *

- *I should always make the correct decision about managing this illness—without bothering the physician too much.*

This exercise might take a few tries before you silence the "censor" inside you and the answers start flowing freely. Do this until you feel like you've got a body of answers that accurately describes your overall answer to each question.

Then—and only then—sit back and look at your list. Discuss the answers with your partner. Ask which answers come from the "Parent" inside you, the "Child," and the "Adult." If you feel uncomfortable with an answer, ask where—or who—it might have come from. On the basis of your own experience, decide which answers are realistic and useful. Ask which answers could be changed, and which could be discarded.

Remember: Our purpose is not to dictate which lines from your script are right for you. We only want you to get your current script on the table and read it with a red pencil in hand. Remember, too, that your self-confidence relates to how realistic—and flexible—your script is.

Chapter Four

· ·

THE CRUCIAL FACTOR: YOUR CHILD'S SELF-CONFIDENCE

Oddly enough, many parents are sure they love their children, but somehow their youngsters fail to get the message. Such parents have not been able to communicate their love. The important thing to understand is: It is the child's feeling about being loved or unloved that affects how he will develop.

As it is with love, so it is with feeling worthwhile. You must know how the message that he is competent and has something to offer others gets across. Then it, too, can become an integral part of his self-picture.
　　　　　　　　　　　　　　　　—Dorothy Briggs, *Your Child's Self-Esteem*

Even people who agree that a child needs healthy self-confidence may not remember that self-esteem is learned. Our children are not blessed with it merely by being born. Your words and actions are important in building that self-confidence.

In Chapter 3, we talked about your self-confidence as a parent. This chapter is also about self-confidence—your child's self-confidence. What can you do to nurture that fragile sense of self-caring in your child? Specifically, when do children feel loved and valued? When do your children feel they're worth being loved and valued?

How Your Words and Actions Build Self-Confidence

Parents' reactions to disease and disability have the greatest impact on how well the child accepts the disease. If parents have positive attitudes, these transfer to the child. Conversely, if parents have negative attitudes such as fear, anger, or denial, these, too, transfer to the child and will have a great impact on a child. Our most "successful" families in diabetes management are those where both parents have genuinely positive attitudes and approaches. The "I can do it" attitude is contagious and affects the whole family.

You've been teaching your child about self-confidence since she was an infant. And that teaching doesn't have to take place in words such as "I think you're great" or "I like what you did today." In fact, you teach self-confidence by the tone of your voice, the character of your gestures, the look in your eyes, and the quality of your attention.

That translates into some specific behaviors:

• Responding to your child in infancy: When your child has dirty diapers, you're there—armed with wet wipes and concern. When he's hungry, you feed him; when he cries, you comfort him.

• Encouraging your child to explore her home environment, encouraging her to dress herself, letting her answer the doorbell and the phone.

• Setting limits that strike the right balance, protecting your child from danger while allowing him to explore, satisfy his curiosity, and sharpen his skills.

• Letting your child know, in advance, about the challenges to be faced: The first permission to leave the house without you; the first day of school; the first test and homework assignment; the first time behind the wheel; the first date, and the first job.

• Supporting your child in her activities—a kind of "parenting as spectator sport." This implies faithful attendance at school plays, ball games, band concerts, and scout meetings.

• Encouraging your child to make friends and welcoming those friends into your home.

• Letting your child take on more responsibility, assigning tasks that are "right" for each age level: cleaning the bedroom, mowing the lawn, running errands for you, caring for a sibling, and so on.

• Praising your child for work well done; consoling your child when things don't go well. Sensing when it's okay to tease her, and avoiding sarcasm about how your child looks, sounds or feels.

No one does all these things all the time, and you can't always expect to do any of them perfectly. The crucial question is this: Does your child feel that you're "there" when it counts? And do you truly want to be there? When you ask yourself this question, try to answer it from your child's viewpoint–not your own. It's not what you know about this that counts; it's what your child feels.

Underlying Attitudes Matter

We've briefly mentioned some of the things you can say or do to build and sustain your child's self-confidence. Usually those behaviors are simple outward expressions of a few basic attitudes.

Your attitudes are complicated, of course, and they shift over time. But what's essential to these basic attitudes can be summed up in a few simple sentences:
  • "I like living and I like myself."
  • "My child deserves my attention and time."
  • "I'll keep my promises to my child."
  • "I'll separate self-worth from test results."
  • "I'll work with my partner to agree on appropriate behavior for our child."
  • "I'll say what I need to say, but I won't make my child feel shame."
  • "Once in a while, I'll try to see the world from my child's viewpoint."
  • "I'll set limits for my child's behavior, and I'll make sure her behavior falls within those limits. When it does, I'll praise my child."
  • "I'll let my child grow up."

Liking life, your child–and yourself. How does a child learn that life itself is worth living?

Through explanations? ("Remember, son, each day is a new opportunity, and you've got something special to give.")

Through philosophizing? ("Actually, ask yourself if the question itself has any meaning.")

Through "greeting card" cliches? ("Today is the first day of the rest of your life.")

Probably none of these. Actually, your child forms an answer from her own observation and experience. In the early years, that means observing you.

Even though he can't say it in so many words, your child is asking from the beginning, "Do the most important adults in my life enjoy being alive?" And even if you aren't putting your response in so many words, you are answering the question.

How? Through your actions. Through your tone of voice. Through your energy level and enthusiasm. Through the way you greet your child in the morning. Through the way you use your leisure time, the way you express affection, the way you deal with disappointment, the way you react to your child's chronic illness, and in a thousand other ways.

In short, if you like life, you'll communicate that fact to your child. You can't help but communicate it, actually. And if your attitude toward life is one of basic distrust, of merely bearing up under suffering, of living only to fulfill duty and obligation—your child will learn that soon enough.

The same comments apply to liking yourself. For more help on this point, see Chapter 3.

Giving your time and attention. Actually giving your time and attention is one expression of an even deeper stance toward life: "I like having a child."

Think back to your decision to have children. Was this a conscious choice for you? Did your child just "come along"? Did you always assume you would have children—no questions? Or did you bring a child into the world because people expected you to? Did you ever imagine yourself the parent of a chronically ill child?

Those of us who became parents in the '70s and '80s were perhaps the first generation to really question whether or not we should have children and if so, how many. We were able to ask "What do I want out of life anyway, and how does a child fit into the picture?"

Many people answered in clear and definite ways–again, not so much in words as in actions: Delaying families in order to establish careers. Deciding and accepting that mother would work outside the home. Hiring one or more people to take care of children–day-care providers, long-term babysitters, part-time or full-time nannies. Each decision is a response to our basic question.

In reality, you probably asked yourself this question many times, and your response may have changed over the years. Do you know people such as:

• The married couple who remained a couple for 10 years before deciding to start a family?

• The feminist who, at one point, vowed never to have children or to marry, then decided that childrearing could fit with her political outlook?

• The people who decided that careers and free time always came first–until they started to approach the "end" of the childbearing years?

• The woman who got her MBA, who paid her dues to land a job in management, who "topped out" in the corporate world–and then climbed off the career ladder to raise a child?

• The men and women who opt for "alternative families," extended families, and step-families? This includes single-parent families, those who gained child custody after divorce, those who remarried and gained stepchildren, and those who chose to raise children outside of conventional marriage.

In short, parents in the last 20 years made their decisions about having children in the midst of change–changes in society and personal change. The "flower children," the "now generation," the "yuppies"– each era brought with it distinct ideas about the value and nature of parenthood.

This change has been positive: In many cases, people had children not because they felt obligated, or because everyone else did, but because they really wanted children. When women entered the work force in greater numbers, they had to think seriously about the place of children in their lives, about the time it would take away from personal and professional commitments. When these women and their families did bring children into the world, it was a matter of conscious choice.

Still, some new complications arose. First among them is the "super-woman syndrome"—those women who want it all. Can you see this ideal woman in your mind's eye? She is the person with time to juggle marriage, full-time career, two children, aerobics classes, tennis lessons, volunteer work, daily exercise, cooking, and household chores. What's more, she can do it all with unflagging energy and seemingly good cheer.

Dads may face a similar problem. Traditionally, their role has been to conquer the outside world, to be the main provider, to manage the money, to keep the cars running, and to keep every machine in the house in good working order. To this has been grafted another ideal— the "sensitive" man, the man who shares child-rearing chores equally with the woman and who expresses his affection and emotions openly to his family.

Both roles—supermom and superdad—are really only the fiction of glamour magazines, soap operas, and talk shows. The problem, however, arises when many women and men measure themselves against these standards—or against some others equally impossible to achieve.

People who are very busy must ask themselves: When can we give children our time and full attention? What is the place of children in our lives? Can we manage children only with the help of full-time day care and two live-in nannies? Does mom or dad choose to stay at home, sacrificing the career climb for now? Or do we choose something between these two extremes?

Children actually don't want your full attention all the time—nor is this ideal. And, as we pointed out in Chapter 2, there's more to life than raising children. Parents need personal and private time, too.

Our purpose is not to answer these questions—or to make anyone feel guilty. It is simply to convince you to ask the question: "When does my child really receive my undivided attention?" Also, "What does the way I spend my time tell my children about how important they are?"

Keeping your promises. Any friendship—between parent and child, between friends, between lovers—is founded on promises. "I promise to keep time open for you." "I promise to listen when you need to talk." "I promise to try and work things out if I get angry or frustrated with you." These are just a few of the promises needed to sustain any relationship that's more than just a temporary convenience.

Your relationship with your child is also based on promises. There are promises to take vacations, to fix a special meal, to be a spectator at ball games, to help with homework. And, if your child has a chronic illness, there's another layer of promises – that you'll comfort and console, manage medication, explain what's going on, provide transportation to the doctor's office, and be a steady, loving presence during crises.

Obviously, it's important to keep these promises to your child – or to explain thoroughly and ask forgiveness when you have to break one. And it's very important to make certain that you don't break promises frequently. Doing this lets your child know in certain terms: "I'm important. I'm worth making time for."

Speaking to your child with one voice. What happens when you and your partner disagree about the limits for a child's behavior? Aside from confusion on everyone's part, there's also damage to your child's self-confidence. You may want a child who will express every fear about chronic illness, while your spouse may value the child who "takes it in stride." Given these mixed messages, your child simply cannot win.

Avoiding shame. Below is a list of statements – things parents typically say to children. These statements are grouped in pairs. In each pair, the statements basically convey the same content, but they imply different attitudes toward the child:

- "I feel worried because it seems you're not eating enough."
- "You're impossible to feed."

* * *

- "Would you please pick up your room a little more?"
- "You're sloppy."

* * *

- "If you turn in your homework late, you'll have to live with the consequences."
- "You'll never amount to anything as a student."

- "Are you feeling okay? It seems to me that you have a pretty low energy level right now."
- "I think you're just being lazy."

* * *

- "I got mad when you wandered away from me at the park. I was afraid of losing you."
- "Don't ever leave my sight again. You're a bad little girl. Sometimes I wish I'd never had children."

You get the idea. In each pair, the first statement focuses mainly on your reactions, your feelings about something your child has done. In contrast, the second statement judges—even shames—the child. These statements not only say something about how the child behaved in a certain situation, but they tell the child, "I think you'll always disappoint or anger me in any situation."

We can put this another way. The first statement in each pair is an "I" message: "I'm concerned . . . ." "It seems to me . . . ." "I get worried when . . . ." These state something about you without condemning the child. They still let you set limits, but they also let your child know you care.

We can call the second statements "you" messages. "You are a bad little girl." "You will never amount to anything." "You are just lazy." Can you imagine how 20 years of such messages affect a child? Some people have called it giving the child a "shame-based identity." Perhaps you know something about this from your own experience. In any case, a shame-based identity is not an appropriate legacy for any child.

Using "I" statements is an essential communication skill for parents—maybe the most essential one. If you're not good at turning "You" statements into "I" statements, take heart: This is something you can learn and improve on.

Another point is relevant here: Your child deserves the same respect you would give another adult. For example, most of us take pains to avoid embarrassing our friends in public; yet we may not be so careful with our own children. Imagine that you're eating out with a group of people and someone spills a glass of water all over the table. Chances are you'd ignore the incident or offer a sympathetic comment. But, if your child does the same thing after you've had a really rotten day at work, do you resort to shaming? "We just can't take you anywhere, can we?" Our children deserve more than this.

Seeing the world from your child's viewpoint. It's standard advice to tell new parents: "Get down on your knees or on the floor sometimes. Talk to your child at his eye level." You may have heard this many times—more often than you care to. Still, it's good advice.

We'd like to extend it a little more: "Now that you're at eye level, stay there a little while and see how the world appears to your child."

Think about it: What does life look like to your child? Here are some statements from parents who answered this question:

My four-year-old probably sees a world where these big, towering people we call adults are in control. She's absolutely dependent on these big people for food, clothing, and support. Still, she really doesn't understand these big people—why they say what they do, what they'll do next.

Not being able to predict what will happen next, just waiting for things to happen—I really don't know what that's like. I really think it frustrates her.

* * *

I take for granted many items of common sense and I assume my child knows these things too. But I shouldn't really do this. For instance, he asked me the other morning if today was a day-care day (a Monday through Friday) or a stay-at-home day (a Saturday or Sunday). He asks me this question all the time.

But suddenly it occurred to me: What would it be like to wake up in the morning and have no idea where you were going after you got dressed? I wonder if this gives him a sense of adventure—or a sense of anxiety?

* * *

Our little girl is a preschooler who loves to play and spread out her dolls all over the house. She also likes to build "forts"—tables and chairs and stacks of pillows covered with blankets, like a crude tent. I get mad at her sometimes because I'm a real neatnik: I guess I live by the old saying, "A place for everything and everything in its place." Then I come home from work and see her ramshackle tents all over the house!

But how is she to know the "place" for each thing? Have we ever told her? To me, each item in the house belongs in a certain place. That's more the way I see things, I guess. It's easy to forget that kids divide up space differently from grownups.

* * *

The other night I came home after a horrendous day at work. Nothing had gone right that day – one of those days that you're just glad you got away from the office without breaking anything. At home, our son, a five-year-old, is crying about losing his puppy. This is a stuffed animal he's had forever, it seems. Now this child has a room filled with these animals – stuffed rabbits, cows, pigs, dogs, you name it. There must be 20 of them on the shelves in his room.

I'd had it that night, and I kept thinking to myself, "Why doesn't he just take another one?" They're all basically alike, anyway. How trivial it seemed to get so upset over a thing like this.

But then he reminded me that toys aren't all alike. And I'm sure that's true for him. Each animal has its own personality, its own special place in his heart. I forget that these are a big part of his world. When he loses a puppy, he probably feels the way I do when I lose an account at work.

Now, put this book down for a minute and try the following exercise. After doing so, you may understand a lot more about your child.

Think about your child's schedule on a typical weekday. What time does she get up? What's the first thing she does after getting up? If your child is very young, who decides what she'll wear that day? Does she get dressed herself, or does she depend on someone else for that? How do you think this makes her feel?

Do this for each event in the child's day – getting dropped off at day care, walking to school, taking a test, choosing sides for a ball game, coming home, taking medication, visiting the doctor, getting seated for dinner, looking for friends to play with.

In your imagination, be as detailed and precise as you can. Try to see the sights as your child sees, and to hear the voices he hears. Walk right into the child's world. First, see him doing each activity. Then try to imagine how he reacts to each event: What is your child thinking, feeling, or saying right now?

To do this exercise, you may need to ask your child a lot of questions about what he does each day. This is useful in itself, and it alone can make you feel closer. We are continually surprised at the number of parents who simply have no idea what their children do during the day.

Setting limits and accepting your child. Parents are often deluged with wonderful-sounding advice. Much of it seems, however, to boil down to two ideas:

• Love your child unconditionally. Praise your child often. Don't judge, blame, or criticize.

• Set limits for your child's behavior. Enforce those limits: When your child's behavior falls outside those limits, then be firm about the consequences.

To many people, these statements seem to come from different worlds. Typical reactions follow:

How can I set limits without criticizing my child?

* * *

I'd like to be firm, but that makes me a judge of my child's behavior, doesn't it?

* * *

What does the word "unconditional" mean, anyway? There are times when I'm downright mad or disappointed at my child, and I need to let her know. I wonder if any of these psychologists have ever raised kids.

Indeed, it sounds almost as if you'd have to be two different people to follow this advice. One person would love, cuddle, and praise all the time. The other would be an emotional traffic cop—keeping lists of rules, monitoring misbehavior, and laying down the law.

Yet, these two basic statements—"be loving" and "be firm"—really do work together. They express the fundamental balance you have to strike as a parent. It may be hard to find this balance in theory, but we can find it in practice.

The philosopher and psychologist William James wrote about this kind of balance. Take these two statements:

"People are all pretty much the same."

and

"Everyone is different."

James once overheard an uneducated craftsman reconcile these seeming opposites. The carpenter said this: "There are not many differences between people. But the differences that do exist are important." This simple man, James said, had summed up volumes of psychology in two terse sentences.

Can we find a similar way to balance the ideas "be firm" and "be loving"? Try this:

• Set fair, clear limits for your child's behavior. Let your child know the consequences of going outside those limits:

"You agreed to babysit Tom. If you're not here on time, no more Friday night movies."

• When your child's behavior falls within those limits, accept his behavior unconditionally. Praise the thing your child does well:

"You did a great job caring for Tom." (Refrain from mentioning, however, that the house is messy.)

• When behavior falls outside the limits, enforce the consequences. But when you do so, avoid shaming the child. Let your child know that you're displeased with a certain behavior—not with her as a person.

"You were late for your appointment to babysit for Tom, and that made me late for my business appointment. Your tardiness was not deliberate meanness, I know, just thoughtless. But, we had a deal."

Let your child grow up. Giving your child appropriate responsibility is a sure way to boost self-confidence. Examples are easy to find in daily life: letting your child dress and bathe himself, make the bed, clean his room, do yardwork, and do the laundry. Your job as a parent is to choose the right task for your child—one that the child can reasonably handle, but one without disastrous consequences if the child doesn't succeed right away.

Remember, too, that "if at first you don't succeed," principle. Say your child tries dressing herself for the first time. You leave her alone to do this, and when you return, she looks like the Scarecrow from the Wizard of Oz. What you say and do at this point is crucial. Praise her attempt, then calmly explain what went wrong and offer to help. Avoid negative comments. And, most importantly, let her try again tomorrow.

This principle extends to self-care for your child's chronic illness. Sit down with your health care provider and decide what tasks your child can safely manage—and when. If, for example, your child has diabetes, when can he make his own snacks? Or, say you're dealing with asthma or a seizure disorder, when can your child be responsible for managing her own medication? These questions are worth tackling right away.

Sadly, some parents confuse a child's worth with the results of a test that monitors his chronic illness. This might be a physical exam or a blood sugar test, for example. The child feels "worthy" when test results are normal and "worthless" when they're not. Remember: Test results are not barometers of value; they are information to help manage a chronic illness.

Also remember, if parents have a positive and confident attitude that *they* will be able to learn about medications, treatments, signs of real emergencies, and how to talk to their child and the health care team, then this attitude will transfer to the child. The child learns most from his parents. He learns about confidence, and how to make the most of every day. He learns to risk failure by trying new things. He knows he's competent even though all ventures don't turn out to be roaring successes, because you have loved him unconditionally and disciplined him without criticizing.

Chapter Five

· ·

GENERAL
POINTS ABOUT
DEVELOPMENT

W *hen Nels was seven and Chris-
tian three, both sons became diabetic within eleven months of
each other. That was more than twelve years ago and, looking back, I
can see how my husband's and my determination to give our sons independence guided our parenting.*

*There have been problems and frustrations, but there have also been
joys which is really what parenting is all about—diabetes or no. For example, in the grade school years, both boys became aware of peers and
the concept of "normalcy." They had many ideas about the meaning of
"normal." It was eating cotton candy at the fair, having ice cream on
an outing, buying treats at the corner store after school. It was not diabetes.*

*My husband and I explained that many of us are not "normal" by one
definition or another. True, they couldn't eat the lollipops given out by
the bank teller. But, we explained they could do well at school, take part
in sports, develop musical or artistic talents, have friends, and do
hundreds of things that others do to feel good about themselves.*

Janice B. Johnson, *"A Mother's View,"*
Diabetes Forecast, September/October, 1981.

It's easy to get hung up on the specifics of your child's chronic illness,
whether it's asthma, diabetes, seizure disorder, or some other chronic
condition. And, with a daily round of medication, visits to the doctor,

trips to various specialists, insurance coverage and money worries, it's no wonder you sometimes lose perspective.

One result of this is that you tend to forget the big picture, the broad view of your child's progress in growth and development. Nature has arranged things so that human beings develop in an orderly and predictable way. Most of the time, you can expect certain skills to be mastered in a certain order. While each child differs from every other, there are some definable milestones that we can anticipate in every case. These range from the child's first independent steps to the first day at school to, ultimately, the first job and eventual adulthood.

Parents, therefore, by learning something about each milestone, can know:

- What behavior to expect generally at each age level;
- What skills your child can be expected to master and when;
- How much independence it is wise to grant at each stage in your child's development; and
- How any chronic condition is likely to affect your child's developmental progress.

With this information, you can prepare for each milestone in your child's life and you can ask appropriate questions if you are concerned that development is being delayed. Further, you can satisfy your child's key needs at each stage of development, enabling your child to avoid a common problem: that of becoming an adult who is still negotiating life with a child's set of unmet needs. And, you can make smarter decisions in a hundred practical matters.

You won't be likely, for example, to expect a seven-year-old with a seizure disorder to understand the details of brain chemistry, or a three-year-old with diabetes to fully understand and explain food exchanges. Though the eventual aim is to create a person who can manage a chronic illness independently, this goal has to be approached in appropriate stages.

Looking at your child's life as a whole has another advantage: It can comfort you at crucial times. It's easy to despair when your teenager returns from the hairdresser with the latest fashion in hair cuts—something that makes her look like a refugee from a Satanic cult. At that moment, it helps you to know that the story hasn't ended yet. Your child will change. True, she has to rebel in some ways, but that's all part of separating from you and becoming her own person. But it can be heartening to remember that this is a stage and it won't last forever.

Sydney Harris, a syndicated columnist, writes that one day each of us will wake up with the sudden realization: "I am more like my parents than I ever dreamed possible." Perhaps you've already experienced this and, in a capsule, this is the broad picture we're talking about. More likely than not, your children will adopt your basic values and outlook on life.

Use this information, therefore, but go easy on yourself. There is a potential danger in talking about growth and development if you interpret the information as the unquestionable truth, without variations. Remember: Everyone is unique. Don't expect your child to develop exactly "by the book." Growth and development charts are the result of observations of many children and they attempt to cite trends, stating what is generally true for most of those children observed.

In order to make those general statements, however, charts must gloss over the many differences between children. So when it comes to predicting what any one child will do at a given age—well, that's something not even a textbook on growth can do.

Then, you ask, why is information about growth and development still helpful for you? Think of this information as the outline of a story. When a playwright gets ready to write a play, she drafts an outline. This working plan gives the main points of the various characters and their lives, when they're born, who they care about, what they do, how they take part in the main events of the plot. But, at this point, the playwright really doesn't know exactly what words each character will speak.

In the same way, information on growth and development is a kind of working outline for your child's life. But, your child is still free to write his own lines, add individual gestures, embellish with special flourishes, and even rewrite some of the scenes. Yet, there are some common headings in the basic outline.

Keep in mind, too, that looking at "normal" growth and development does not mean believing that your child is just like every other child. On the contrary, knowing how your child differs from the norm can give you an even greater sense of his uniqueness.

We've already determined that knowing about development can make you a more effective mentor and counselor for your child. How? By helping you remember when your child is ready to handle particular tasks. Further, we've learned that knowing about development helps you remember that situations encountered at various ages will pass. Also, knowing that certain problems are "inevitable" keeps you from putting yourself down as a parent. Remember that one of the prime tasks of an adolescent is to assert independence from you—even when it means outright rebellion. When you experience this, you can respond without blaming yourself or your child.

Growth does not always happen in a straight line. While the general direction is forward, there may be some detours and backtracking along the way. For example, consider a fourth-grade boy we know who excels on the playground and is always the first person picked for a football or basketball game. This makes him a peer leader in his age group, and others look to him for approval. Yet, when his class went on an overnight camping trip, he had to confess: "I'm afraid of the dark, and I need my teddy bear."

Psychologists might call this behavior "regression," a return to an earlier stage of childhood. Almost always regression is temporary and nothing to worry about. In fact, you can expect it when your child faces stress—the first time at day care, the first day of school, the first time you talk about what it means to have a chronic illness. Only in the rare event that regression becomes a long-term pattern is there cause for any concern.

What's "normal" is fairly well defined at first—but this changes as children get older. You see this easily if you think for a minute. Take two newborn babies, for example. Barring any major physical disability, we can say that these two children are much alike. They both have certain reflexes and certain immediate needs, which are pretty similar. We can, therefore, meaningfully talk about what's "normal" for an infant.

In contrast, take two sixteen-year-olds. True, we know that these children are facing similar tasks: forging a sexual identity, preparing for adulthood, getting ready to choose a direction in life. But, at this age, each child has infinitely more options than the newborn, and each will resolve life's basic problems in a unique way. At this point, we have to broaden our view of what's "normal" and pay more attention to individual differences.

Ask your health care team how chronic illness will affect your child's growth and development. Children with chronic illness may vary in how fast they "develop" emotionally due to the additional stresses and events they must experience as a result of that illness. Some children seem to master independence very quickly, while others are delayed in their ability to separate from their parents. Use the child's age as a general reference point as you learn about development. When your child's development seems either too fast or too slow, talk to your health care team about your observations and concerns.

In the following chapters, we outline the life story by looking at the child in five stages: infant, toddler, preschooler, school-aged child, and adolescent. More specifically, we highlight two kinds of growth in each stage—physical development and personality development. More information on the topic is offered in the section titled "Resources" at the back of the book. Before you begin, remember: There will be times when what the "textbook" says is not accurate for your child.

Chapter Six

· ·

THE INFANT—
BIRTH TO 1 YEAR

Your child's growth rate is faster during the first year than at any other period in life. A doubling of birth weight generally occurs by the age of 5 months; by 1 year, birth weight triples. The infant's length increases about 50 percent during the first year, and the infant's large muscles begin to work together, helping the child control and direct movement. At age 3 or 4 months, a child can usually lift her head while lying on her tummy; she sits independently and turns her head all directions by 7 months.

Along with all this come some other fantastic accomplishments: By age one, the child can sit anywhere, stand up, stoop, climb, and many even walk.

Eating and sleeping patterns vary. Milk and solid food intake changes dramatically during the first year of life. At two months, the infant drinks 24 to 35 ounces of milk at three- to four-hour intervals, possibly round the clock. By age 6 months, he has probably started on solid foods—including cereal and some fruits. By age 1, the infant moves from eating every three to four hours to a mealtime schedule similar to regular family mealtimes.

By age 10 months, he is usually ready to go off the bottle and use a cup. Children insist on feeding themselves and start using a spoon by age 1. At this age, an infant also begins eating three meals a day, with juices and small, simple snacks taken between meals. He may, at this time, be taken off infant foods in favor of some regular table foods.

By age 1, the infant often changes from sleeping most of the day to being awake most of the day. Nighttime sleeping averages eight to ten hours. In addition, she takes one afternoon nap of two to three hours, and perhaps takes a morning nap if she is an early riser.

Managing the care routine. Administering medication, especially those taken by injection, may be a little harder as the baby gains in strength. Grouchiness, irritability, and unexplained crying may be the only signs of a condition that needs attention, such as low blood sugar.

Still, regular care routines may be essential, even at this early age. For example, with diabetes, daily blood sugar monitoring is important to gauge the infant's insulin and food requirements.

During the first year of a child's life, immunizations are begun and should occur throughout childhood on a regular schedule. Ask your health care provider to make this schedule clear to you. Some infants have no physical reactions to immunizations, while others are irritable and tired for up to 5 days following an immunization.

The infant's personality. As your infant becomes more responsive to your face, voice, and moods, you recognize that your baby smiles at you, laughs with you, gets angry with you. In addition, she may become cool toward strangers.

Around 9 to 12 months, your infant recognizes that your face and voice are not the same as all faces. She does not always want to go to people she does not know. By age 1, the child's world enlarges beyond mother and father. Developing a trusting relationship with another person can be very important during this time.

There's intellectual growth, too, as the child masters a few words by age 1. These include syllables that come to be associated with food, toys, and familiar faces. He also displays joy in learning and discovering simple things.

Caring for the Infant

Promoting your infant's physical health. Common childhood illnesses can affect and be affected by your child's chronic illness. For example, infections generally will raise blood sugar, which requires a change in medication or diet, or both, in infants with diabetes. Also, chronic illness can increase the frequency of common childhood illnesses. When chronic illness is not well managed, the child is more likely to get more infections, get sick more often, be more seriously sick, and stay sick longer.

If you are concerned about any aspect of your child's growth, development, or general health, check with your doctor. As a usual procedure, infants should visit the pediatrician and health care team every two to three months, having weight and length checks at each visit.

Working for good nutrition. Nutrition is a big concern for many parents of children with chronic conditions. Breast feeding or formula for the first 4 to 6 months every three to four hours is generally sufficient. Adding solid foods two or three times a day is often recommended at about 6 months. Special foods or formulas may be prescribed, or omitted, by your health care team. Keeping the diet fairly consistent and on a schedule may be a very important aspect of your child's health care plan.

Amounts, however, cannot usually be controlled. Expecting an infant to eat or drink a precisely weighed or measured meal is unrealistic. Rather, spreading a well-balanced diet over 6 to 8 feedings daily is more feasible. You should discuss the meal plan carefully with your health care team at scheduled visits. Weight and length gains that follow a normal growth curve are good proof that the child is eating the right amount.

It is impossible in the scope of this book to give any detailed instructions for feeding your infant. Two things, however, apply for nearly all parents: 1. Your baby's natural appetite is dependable and controls how much he is going to eat. While daily intake may vary, things usually "average" out over a week's time. 2. To pacify and reward your infant, try holding, cuddling, and the use of a pacifier. Avoid the constant use of juices or food to comfort. The association between food and comfort is hard to break once established. This also means avoiding giving your infant a bottle in bed. Try to hold your baby whenever you feed him.

Become open to your feelings and gain a sense of competence and confidence. Come to understand your own feelings and fears about your infant's care routine. Sometimes treating your child's chronic illness means doing things, such as giving insulin injections or drawing blood samples, that seem at odds with loving your baby. You know that providing insulin really is an act of love, but penetrating the baby's soft skin with a needle is almost too much for you to bear.

Remember: Your baby will learn to be fearful or upset about daily testing if he senses you are. Your attitudes affect your child more than your words and even your behavior.

The best approach to dealing with your feelings is to fully admit that you are experiencing them. The whole idea of a chronic illness may be new to you, but the care routine really will get easier. It just takes a little time. Be kind to yourself and allow time for mental and emotional adjustment.

To help make that adjustment easier, learn as much as you can about your child's illness and the care routine. When you master the facts, you understand the reasons for injections, medication, surgery, or any other care that might seem invasive to your child. Eventually this will increase your comfort level. And, if you don't fully understand the reason for a particular treatment, ask about it and keep asking until you do clearly understand.

You are not expected to become an expert parent in the first year of your baby's life—or in the next 20 years either for that matter. Be patient with your own learning and with your baby's learning. Any chronic illness calls on you to learn a great deal. You will learn, but it does not come all at once.

It's equally important to get emotional support from someone who is significant to you—if not a spouse, then a parent, physician, friend, or another good listener. Fully admit your fears or doubts about the daily routine of caring for an infant with a chronic illness. The best way to deal with these feelings is to become fully aware of them and then to talk about them in a supportive environment.

The security of a schedule. A regular schedule of mealtimes and bedtimes during this first year is an important goal. Your child needs this, because it comforts her to know what to expect and when to expect it. Consistency will make your job as a parent easier. The schedule is probably the most important aspect of the health care plan for some illnesses.

Remember, infants and toddlers should respond to your family's routine and schedules. Unless medically necessary, you should not change everything and everyone to conform to your child's schedule. Sometimes it seems easier to keep peace by fixing meals every two hours, but in the long run, it will be easier and more healthy for your baby to make his schedule conform to your routines. And, if your routines need some improvement, now is a good time to start.

Promoting your infant's emotional health. One of the greatest joys of being a parent is watching the unfolding of your child's personality. Smiles and laughter are the first expression of this. Return these expressions with your own joy. It is worth stopping your busy day for this experience. Use his laughter and funny faces as an excuse to laugh and to brighten your life.

Handling stranger anxiety. Stranger anxiety is normal. Actually, it can be a positive sign that a meaningful relationship has formed between you and your baby. Tell grandparents and babysitters about this behavior and don't let it stop you from getting some time away from baby. Give suggestions for how to hold and comfort the baby and be sure to ask grandparents or babysitters to use things other than food to comfort and soothe.

If, however, your baby is comfortable with strangers, don't be alarmed. There are many other ways she can show you that you are the most important person in her life.

Build a positive world. Repeat the sounds and words you hear your baby say. It helps him to hear and makes the words a part of his vocabulary and it opens the verbal communication between you. Listen carefully to the words you use to describe injections, medication, food items and other aspects of the care routine. Make sure they have a positive meaning whenever possible. Pay attention, also, to the tone of your voice and be aware of any tension in your body that might come with those words. True, things such as shots and blood testing can cause your infant to feel some pain, but you can help defuse any anxiety if you build positive associations with each aspect of the care routine. Be organized; have equipment ready; give injections or draw blood in a well lit, comfortable area; complete the routine quickly, and move on to more pleasant activities.

Return your baby's unconditional love with yours. Don't judge yourself guilty or your child inferior because of chronic illness. Neither of you has anything to justify, anything to apologize for. Many parents harbor an unconscious guilt, struggling with vague feelings that they are somehow to blame for the child's illness. It's as if these parents feel personally responsible for the gene pool. If this applies to you, remember: The origin of much chronic illness is still a mystery to medical science, and most chronic illnesses result from a combination of many factors.

Chapter Seven

THE TODDLER– YOUR CHILD FROM 1 TO 2½ YEARS

How toddlers grow. During the toddler stage, growth slows from the dramatic increases of the first year. Between 1 and 2½ years, the child will gain about five to six pounds and grow four to six inches. All primary teeth are present by 2½ to 3 years and appetite becomes much more variable.

A typical meal plan usually consists of three small meals and three snacks throughout the day. The toddler eats a wide variety of table foods, and, for the most part, can do a pretty efficient job of self-feeding.

Your child becomes more agile physically during this period. Talking, running, and jumping are part of his new repertory of skills.

Many toddlers become dry between 2 and 3 years of age. Signs of readiness for toilet training include: three to four hours of dryness between wet diapers; the ability to tell you he is wet or has to use the bathroom; and the toddler's ability to undress and dress with some help. Also required are your time and willingness to work closely with your toddler to master this new skill.

The toddler's personality. Paired with all this physical development is striking intellectual development. The child further masters language, using simple words, then moving on to groups of words. Keep in mind that your child may say "no" to any question, when he really means both "yes" and "no."

Imitation appears in the child's play. You may notice your child imitating simple tasks that she has seen you do—mixing with a spoon in a bowl, turning on the faucet, washing her hands. She may, at this time, want to play with objects associated with her medical care—the inhaler, the glucose monitor—in the same way she sees you handle them. Allow this explorative play, but make sure it takes place in a safe way.

The downside of this imitation is that toddlers can also learn unhealthy behaviors from their parents and others around them, so be alert for this.

The toddler is not yet able to share or let another child play with toys he believes are his own. Toddlers need to "own" before they can "share."

Testing your limits. Almost continually, toddlers test the limits of their parents. Expect your child to assert her rights and to have a say of her own. This affects medication routines and mealtimes. In addition, your toddler may resist anything associated with bedtime. This will be the hour that he wants more TV, more stories, or more snacks—anything to postpone bedtime.

Handling criticism—but not gracefully. With the toddler period comes strong attachments to parents and other consistent caregivers. Most two-year-olds get upset when parents scold them, and their feelings are easily hurt by criticism or harsh-sounding words. Language helps them deal with this. You may hear your child say, "No, mommy bad girl," or, during play, hear her recite her version of the rules you've been trying to teach her.

Stranger anxiety. "Stranger anxiety" continues with this age group, carrying over from infancy. Toddlers frequently become fearful of physicians and other people in white coats. Why? Because these people are strangers. Your child may learn that "doctor" means shots and blood draws, or other such discomforts.

Curiosity. The toddler is curious. He will try everything in his quest for independence. Such curiosity permits toddlers to discover, interact with, and control their immediate environments. At this age, your child is developing a sense of self and of autonomy. He'll have his own ideas about what he'll want to do and not do, and about what belongs to him.

This is complicated by a limited understanding of time: He still has no idea of what "soon" means.

Dependency. Toddlers are still completely dependent upon you and other adults to provide a range of opportunities for play and learning. These must always be provided with safety in mind. You may also find that your child resists some daily routines at this time, including care for his chronic illness. He is doing this to control his environment and to exert his developing sense of power.

Caring for the Toddler

Promoting your toddler's physical health. It's easy to forget one fact about toddlers and infants: You don't have to push them to develop. They are highly motivated from the moment of birth to actively experience their surroundings. What you can do, though, is set reasonable limits to your child's activities, especially those activities that affect physical health.

Insist on following the care routine. You must determine what is safe or dangerous for your child. Within the limits you set, however, allow your toddler to play, experiment, discover, and learn.

If there are two parents in your family, both should learn and try to be comfortable with the daily care routine. Your toddler may express a definite preference for one parent over the other. This is due to a need to control and has nothing to do with the skills of each of you. Let your child choose a parent for a specific action, such as injections or administering medication. However, both of you should be competent with handling the details of his care.

Avoiding bedtime battles. Toddlers need sleep, but bedtime easily becomes an issue. Be clear and consistent when you think it's time for bed. Keep bedtime routines as peaceful and happy as possible. One way to do this is to "warm up" to bedtime with a series of activities that culminate in crawling under the covers: taking a bath, changing into pajamas, reading a story. You can set loving limits by gently and consistently refusing when your child keeps begging for "just one more story."

Eating well. If special nutrition concerns are important to managing your child's chronic illness, be sure to carefully discuss a meal plan with your health care team. When you do, ask about how flexible the plan can be. A logical time to do this is at scheduled visits every three to four months.

With toddlers, as with infants, you and your health care team will look for weight and length gains consistent with your child's potential, comparing them with growth charts for most children of the same age.

As much as possible, model your toddler's eating schedule after the family's mealtimes. Avoid constant snacking as a substitute for regularly scheduled meals. Offer all snacks and meals to your toddler while he is seated in his high chair or at the table. This way, he learns when it is time to eat and when it is time to play. Also, offer snacks that are nutritionally worthwhile. This is the one time you can control what your child eats.

Don't force feed your child. There will be times when she refuses food because her need or desire for food has decreased. When this happens, medication dosage may need to be adjusted. Be sure to discuss this with your health care team.

Adapting to the family routine. Again, expect your toddler to conform to your family routine and schedules as much as possible–not vice versa. Yes, you could let your toddler sleep as late as he chooses and then fix a separate breakfast for him. In the long run, however, it will be easier–and more healthy for your child–to eat on the family schedule. Remember: If the whole family would benefit from changes in the routine, this is an excellent opportunity to make those changes.

Conquering the toilet. Many parents are concerned about what age to start toilet training. While some children are out of diapers by 12 to 15 months of age, others are not ready until after age 3. There is a range of possible times here. If your child has diabetes, remember that urinary frequency and volume can increase when blood sugars are high. If there is a pattern to this, discuss it with your health care team.

Promoting your toddler's emotional health. A healthy, supportive relationship between you and your toddler is one that takes your needs and the child's into account. Balance the needs of your child with the needs of everyone in the household, including parents, brothers, and sisters. Parents, you need time away from your child and the chronic illness. Use this time to nurture your relationship. Schedule some time to be alone–weekly if possible.

Moreover, treat this appointment as you would treat a business or medical appointment: Cancel your private time only when absolutely necessary. Also, teach other important people in your child's life—babysitters, relatives, close friends—about your child's care routine. Doing so can help you build a reservoir of competent help—something that gives you some respite.

Overcoming fear with fair limits. As you do this, avoid feeling sorry for your child. And, don't allow others to feel sorry for your toddler because of chronic illness. This kind of sympathy can incapacitate you and other family members. It can also prevent you from being firm and providing the discipline your toddler really needs. Your child needs strong, secure love—not pity or anguish.

Design the daily routines so there are fair but firm limits on the range of your child's choices. For example, she will have her insulin shot at specific times, although she may choose the site of the injection. She must have the injection; this is not negotiable. Or he can choose green beans or peas as the vegetable at his meal; he cannot choose carrots or squash. Otherwise, you'll spend all your time as a short order cook.

This principle also applies to your visits to your physician. If your toddler suddenly cries when you bring him in for a check-up, don't overreact by rescheduling the appointment or avoiding treatment. Instead, try to do something fun to associate with the visit, such as a trip to the park for play after the appointment. Be firm about your basic expectations. Your toddler's feelings are real, but they will resolve if you don't give in. Try not to reinforce his anxiety with your own.

In short, don't let your fears become your child's fears—or for that matter, don't let your child's fears become yours. Those fears will change as your child gets older. So will your feelings and acceptance of chronic illness.

Loving without judging. Remember to be careful not to place "good" or "bad" values on the results of medical tests and lab procedures. With diabetes, blood glucose numbers are high or low, but children are not good or bad because of those numbers. Sure, it's natural to feel frustrated when results are outside the goals you're working to achieve. Look back briefly on possible reasons for not meeting those goals, but don't get hung up on this. It's more important to look ahead and define the changes you need to make.

Chapter Eight

· ·

THE PRESCHOOLER

How the preschooler grows. Physical growth slows a bit during the toddler years, and this trend continues into the prechooler period (ages 2½ to 5).

You may wonder how any growth takes place, looking at the way your child eats. You're likely to be frustrated by your preschooler's quirky, unpredictable appetite. Your child may even refuse certain foods temporarily. During this age, you're likely to say, "My child lives on nothing but peanut butter and sunshine."

Your child sleeps differently at this age, too. Some preschoolers will go without naps. Perhaps your child consistently woke during the night as an infant and toddler, keeping you up too. You can expect this behavior to taper off, though you may have to deal with a new phenomenon: nightmares. But even if his sleep is interrupted, chances are your preschooler will have plenty of energy the next day.

During these years, your child will master new coordination skills: using scissors, coloring in the lines in books, writing her name. Additionally, preschoolers start dressing themselves.

You can expect that your child will become dry during the day, before she becomes dry at night. Remember, urination is more frequent with some chronic conditions, so this may make toilet training more difficult.

The preschooler's personality. Expect your preschooler to become a more sophisticated thinker. His memory sharpens, too. If you make a promise that involves something the preschooler wants, expect him to remember it—for days—until you deliver.

Putting the world in order. During these years, your child strives to put her world into order. One facet of this is learning to count. Another is becoming sensitive to time: predicting when meals will take place, when you get home from work, and when it's time for bed. Further, the child gains a more accurate sense of space. On a return from a long drive, he'll be able, for example, to tell when you're getting close to your house. Also, he'll be able to recognize the same object, such as the city skyline, from many different angles.

Yet, the preschooler sees the world through the prism of her emotions; logic is not a primary factor at this age. It's almost as if the preschooler thinks you have godlike powers: You should be able to make snacks appear when you're miles from a refrigerator. You should be able to change the weather from cloudy to sunny.

Rules are important to the preschooler, and often he'll repeat things you say. Expect to get a lecture if you drive without fastening your seatbelt—especially when you've just buckled your preschooler into his carseat. Such behavior is part of his attempt to learn and remember what he hears adults say.

"No" is an important word to the toddler, and it remains so to the preschooler. At this age, though, your child may be able to back up any refusal with reasons: "I don't want to;" "You're not nice;" "It's not fair." This may include "no" to the daily care routine also, with refusals to take medication, injections, and to do breathing exercises.

The mean, lean, learning machine. At this age, your child is preparing mentally for the next major intellectual and social event in her life: school. You'll see constant signs of this. For one, she asks questions faster than you can answer them. You may be called upon to repeat answers, and you'll find it challenging to explain the world in a way the preschooler can understand.

Now is the natural time to encourage learning. Reading books, taking trips to the zoo, going on walks in the park—all become a kind of classroom and forum for learning. You may be surprised at how much your child actually remembers and understands.

Your child's emotional life. Another new development is the acquisition of a language to describe feelings. Your child matches names to emotions: "I'm afraid." "I hurt inside." "I feel sad today." "I miss grandma and grandpa."

Fear becomes an emotion of some prominence. The morning news, pictures in the newspaper, violent television programs—these may distress your child. Even some children's books may be frightening. You'll need to become aware of how your child handles all this.

Children worry about injuries during this time, especially those that may affect their chronic condition. The daily care routines, in particular any that "invade" their bodies, such as injections, may turn into crises.

From the mouths of babes. What's more, your child becomes a kind of lay theologian and philosopher. Now you'll start hearing the big questions: "Why do things die?" "Do I have to die?" "Why do people get sick?" "Why am I sick?" Expect questions about God, heaven, and other basic religious terms.

During the preschool years, you'll see patterns in your child's words, actions, and responses—a distinct personality. One of the most important tasks during this time is to forge an identity. Part of this is stating the differences between boys and girls, learning the names for male and female genitals, and sexual curiosity.

"Sexual" play may appear during this time. Although it may seem too early to worry about sexuality, you may need to deal with some of these issues. Occasional sex play and masturbation are common among preschoolers. Ignoring this behavior or treating it lightly is usually the best strategy.

Join the play and watch the artist. Acting is an important part of personality development—playing games where your child takes on the role of father, mother, sister, brother, teacher, doctor, day-care provider, or TV personality. Also common are "dress-up" games: Expect frequent requests to borrow your shoes and repeated invitations for you to join in.

Look at the pictures your child draws during this time. Often these mirror the child's self-image. Chronic illness may alter the pictures children draw of themselves.

Preschoolers often mimic what you do. Children with chronic illness may dramatize situations in which they can be the parent or a sibling without the illness.

Caring for the Preschooler

Promoting your preschooler's physical development. Your preschooler's physical development is progressing in tandem with his developing personality and sense of independence. These are the years when your child constantly challenges you about what food to eat and interrupts your conversations. Battles over when to go to bed may continue from the toddler years.

Indeed, your preschooler seems to have a contradictory attitude toward schedules, in general. She may remain uninterested in meals, languish at the dinner table, and even refuse to eat. If you change the meal schedule, however, she may complain loudly. The preschooler seems to like and dislike routines at the same moment.

Coping with change. These are also the years of less dramatic changes in the rate of growth. Appetites vary. Trust your child's appetite, don't force food, don't coax, keep meals as scheduled, and don't react to swings in appetite or food likes and dislikes.

As we said earlier, most children will master toilet training during these preschool years. Be sure to give your child love and support in this area—especially if his chronic condition poses extra challenges. Help him find the bathroom at his friends' homes and other places you visit. Send a consistent message: "I know you'll learn how to be dry."

You should begin your child's visits to the dentist and a schedule of regular tooth brushing during the preschool years. Routine brushing in these years builds a lifetime of good dental hygiene habits.

As you did during the infant and toddler stages, keep tabs on your preschooler's height and weight gains. It's a good idea to do this every four months. If you don't see any change over an eight-month period, ask your child's doctor about it. If you are at all concerned that your child is overweight or underweight, discuss this with the physician.

Avoiding the big battles. A lot of the work you'll have to do as the parent of a preschooler centers on feeding. Turn off the TV and issue your "meal call," allowing enough time for the child to calm down and get ready to eat. During the meal, try to keep the mood peaceful and pleasant. This is not the time to discipline your child or settle arguments.

Schedule snack times that allow your child to become hungry again for meals. You'll also have to be clear about what snacks are allowed, and when. Try to offer a choice of foods, consistent with your child's meal plan. Remember, though, that it's ultimately your child's responsibility to eat; you can only be held responsible for setting a pleasant tone and presenting the right foods.

Meal times offer you a chance to take advantage of your preschoolers desire to help you. Encourage him to help set the table, serve food, and clean up.

To ease the battles over bedtime, avoid using the bedroom as a place to isolate or punish your child. Be prepared to help your child overcome his fear of the dark or to confront nightmares. Books and television contribute to a greatly expanded fantasy life for your preschooler and some of this activity of the imagination may appear as night fear.

Building self-care. Learning to take care of himself is an ongoing and necessary process for a child with chronic illness. Training for this should begin early, perhaps in the toddler stage, and it should continue throughout the preschool, school-age, and teen years. The goal is to give your child the knowledge, skills, confidence, and sense of purpose needed to take care of himself and his illness. It is never too early to get your child involved in this process. As soon as you sense he's interested, let him make choices about food selection, talk with him about medications, and encourage him to ask questions of his health care team.

Helping your preschooler to learn and love. Despite the developing intellect of the preschooler, don't expect her to really understand the details of her chronic condition. Some unrealistic forms of thinking may carry over from earlier years. "My illness will go away soon if I just wish hard enough." "Maybe this happened because my parents were bad, or because I'm bad." "I'm the only one in my family with this sickness. Maybe I'll never grow up." Be careful not to say anything—even in jest—that encourages any of these views.

Bear in mind that your preschooler may be threatened by any significant change in your routine. Visiting a new physician, seeing the school he'll attend, moving to a new home—all these have the potential to cause serious stress.

What's your child really asking? Your child may try your patience with questions, questions, and more questions. In addition to all the questions you're used to hearing, there will be new and searching questions about the nature of his chronic illness.

Dealing with these questions is often perplexing. You'll need to develop a "third ear" to listen for the "question behind the question." For example, the question, "Where did I come from?" may really mean "If I have an illness, was I born the same way as other kids?" In short, your child may not be looking for facts as much as for reassurance.

Also, it's easy to give too much information, or to give the wrong kind of information. Often your main task is to help your child find the right words to describe his illness—not to provide all the medical details. Provide a kind of working vocabulary that allows him to explain the essentials of his condition. This gives him a sense of mastery and, little by little, reduces the mystery of it all.

Remind your child of the larger picture. One of your biggest challenges during the preschool years is to help your child strike that delicate balance between extremes: cuddliness and defiance, craving for independence and fear of the new, the conflicting desires to grow up and be baby again. All these emotions will be active during the preschool years, so don't be surprised by them. The "work" your child must do during these years is more concentrated and demanding than at any other stage during human life.

A good way for you to respond to all this is to remind your child of the feelings of others. Your preschooler needs help with this because her ability to empathize is as yet undeveloped. Let her know that the limits and rules you insist on are designed to help everyone get along. You don't impose rules because you're angry or tired of the child. For example:

- Sometimes you ask her to be quiet, which allows other people to take part in conversation.
- You keep him to a regular bedtime schedule because you want him to feel refreshed and ready for the next day.
- You work with her to say "please" and "thank you" because you want her to be courteous in social situations.

You are the most important teacher. Take advantage of every opportunity for learning. You can do this in a lighthearted way, without dividing time into "learning time" and "everything else." A visit to the pet shop can become an impromptu lesson in biology and zoology. Straightening up a shell collection can be a chance to practice counting. A trip to the doctor can be a time to learn the names of city streets. If you're lucky, the "child" in you can surface as you watch the world and hear it through your child's experiences. Seize the opportunity!

Don't be overly structured with all this learning, however. Your preschooler's attention span is still limited. It is better to communicate facts briefly and concisely, responding to a question tersely without delivering a lecture.

Talking about illness. You don't have to hide your fears or concerns about the chronic illness you're dealing with. If your child has to enter the hospital, it's okay to admit that you don't have all the answers and that you can't control the outcome. Let him know, however, that he's getting the best care you can provide and that you'll be there when he needs you.

The pitfalls of comparison. As a parent, one instinctive technique you may tend to use at this stage is also one of the most potentially destructive to your child's self-esteem: comparison. As adults many of us do this regularly to ourselves: "I'm 40; I should have accomplished more by now." "At this age, why am I still struggling with questions about what career is right for me?" "Will other people think I'm stupid if I turn down this job offer?"

When dealing with children, comparison takes many forms:
- Your sister is so neat, I wonder what happened to you.
- Your brother always dresses himself so nicely. You could learn from him.
- Of all the children in this block, you are the noisiest.
- Most children your age don't have accidents and wet the bed at night.

Comparing one child to another is something that most parents can—with a little training—learn to recognize and avoid. But another form of comparison is harder to pinpoint: Comparing your preschooler, not with another person, but with an image or an expectation.

For your child's sake—and your own—find a source of motivation other than comparison. You don't have to compete with anyone—even with yourself. Encourage your preschooler to find out what she's interested in and to pursue it for its own sake—not to get one up on anyone else. In the preschool years, that area of interest could be anything from dinosaurs to gardening. You can also help by refusing to use comparison in any form when you talk to your child.

As important as it is for you to set limits, remember to let your guard down once in a while. Apologize when it's appropriate. All of us get angry with our children. Sometimes we lose our tempers. When you're dealing with the anxiety and stress caused by chronic illness, your patience is often strained. It's good to say you're sorry when things get out of hand. Let your child know that you set limits for yourself as well as for her. Explain that you do your best to abide by them, but sometimes you fail.

If you feel angry, exhausted or resentful much of the time, you may need to do than just apologize. The same applies if you are concerned about physically abusing your child. Talk with your health care provider about this and ask for help.

Wishes, magic, and big questions. Earlier we mentioned your preschooler's somewhat magical view of reality: feeling that chronic illness is a punishment for misdeeds; believing that wishing will make the condition disappear. These might surface in comments such as "If I just eat my carrots every day, my asthma will go away," or "If I walk slowly, I'll never have a seizure."

When you hear these, don't worry. They're typical of preschoolers, with or without chronic illness. As often as needed, explain that wishing alone doesn't make things happen.

You'll also hear questions about large, abstract issues such as death, and irrational fears of being abandoned, broken, or hurt. Help your child to see the logical connection between events. Provide emotional reassurance frequently: hugs, "I love you's," and a calm, steady presence. Always reassure your child that you are in this together.

Chapter Nine
. . . .
THE SCHOOL-AGED CHILD

Growth during the early school years. The early school years—ages 5 to 11—hold many treasures for parents. Among them is watching the physical development of your child. Look for the development of distinct facial features, an individual body shape and posture, and increased coordination as your youngster becomes an individual. While the rate of physical growth slows a bit from the dramatic increases in earlier life, children in this age group, on average, grow about two inches each year. Although height increases, the body becomes slimmer.

It is not necessary for your child to eat as much during this period, as his need for calories declines. A related milestone: Your child loses baby teeth and gains new, permanent teeth. This is all part of the physical maturation that continues during the early school years.

Along with this comes a new physical prowess. Now your child enjoys baseball and soccer, rope jumping, and the 50-yard dash. Smaller, finer movements—such as writing—are easier, too.

How personality develops during the early school years. A marked change comes in about the quality of your school-aged child's thinking as she is now able to evaluate alternatives. This means, for example, that she can think through the consequences of going to a neighbor's house without telling you; or she can predict what will happen if she comes home from school an hour late without calling you. Furthermore, when you talk about the consequences of going outside in cold weather without a warm coat, or about riding a bicycle while wearing dress clothes, your child will understand.

Still, it's hard for the school-aged child to carefully think through long-term consequences and to turn understanding into action. You'll still need to set limits.

A related change is a more complete understanding of time. Now you can meaningfully talk about things that will take place in the future. Your child can, as the psychologists say, "delay gratification." For instance, he can understand that saving money from a paper route now makes it possible to buy a new bike in three months.

Opening up to other people. The capacity of the child to feel empathy develops gradually during the early school years. You'll begin to see evidence that your child can understand how others feel, and can see what joy and sorrow mean to another person. This makes deeper friendships possible and your child may well have a close buddy during this time—usually one of the same sex. Despite all this new-found sensitivity, you can still expect some defiance when one of your requests doesn't meet the child's approval, however.

Seeing the world one thing at a time. Although the ability to understand time, evaluate alternatives, and empathize are all developing, your child still thinks on a concrete level. What do we mean by this? Well, that when your child talks about birth, she talks about the birth of one particular baby she knows of—not the birth process in general. Or that when you read a book about pets, she relates the information first to her own pet. Other more abstract ideas—space, the universe, death—may not make much sense at this age, except as they relate to things your child can feel, hear, touch, or see.

Generally this means your child finds it hard to digest information about the long-term consequences of his chronic illness. However, you can talk about short-term consequences of certain behaviors. Examples are failing to follow a prescribed meal plan or forgetting to take medication. You can, with caution, allow children to experience some minor consequences as part of the learning process during this time, but the key word is "caution."

Seeing things in groups. Remember those collections of random objects you always saw in your preschooler's room—rocks, shells, sticks, marbles, baseball cards? During the school years you'll see a change in these collections, one that reflects a growing ability to analyze and group things into categories. Instead of a hodge-podge of stacks, your school-aged child will tend to sort objects according to some organizational scheme: rocks grouped according to colors, sticks grouped according to size, and dolls grouped in "families." Still, don't expect the logic of these groupings to always make sense to you.

Developing a learning style. Your child's learning style and favorite subjects will become apparent during the early school years. Some children will excel at physical education and drama and struggle with reading. Others will learn well through books and discussions but feel ill at ease with creative writing or drawing assignments. Try to become aware of these differences as they emerge.

Observe your child at home: Does he like to analyze and think things through? How does he feel about reading and writing? Does he learn better through manipulating objects and working with his hands? If so, he may prefer art, music, and science labs. Ask your child's teachers about these things and talk about your child's preferred way of learning as you have observed it. Keep in mind, though, that none of these learning patterns are set in stone. Your child's abilities will develop and change for many years to come.

Learning through hobbies. At this age children are likely to use hobbies as an important adjunct to learning. This is the stage for model cars, model railroads, doll houses, soap box derbys, flashy bikes, and Barbies. Sometimes these hobbies cost a good deal of money—which is exasperating for you if they're given up after a short time. Use common sense when spending money for these activities, and remember not to try to compensate for your child's chronic illness by buying expensive toys and hobby items.

Time for 10,000 questions. That endless stream of questions you noticed during your child's preschool years continues as the child goes to school. Sometimes it seems as if the only words your child knows are "why," "what's that," and "how come." She wants to know the name of every tree and wildflower, to know how the car works and why the power lawnmower makes so much noise. You may be a frequent visitor to the library to help her look up all the relevant details on clouds, dinosaurs, rainbows, trains, and bumble bees.

Your child will make more sense of the answers he comes home with—largely because of his increasing mastery of language. If you hear your school-age child talking to himself or repeating phrases under his breath, he is probably trying to process new information.

Language development during these years opens new possibilities for meaningful communication with him, but not all your child's thinking and speaking is reality-based. He may still wonder if dreams are real, or wish that his chronic illness would just go away. At times you will still have to remind him that his illness is not a punishment for something he has done or said and that it will not go away.

The little bureaucrat. Your child may not get any prizes for flexible thinking during the early school years. Rules are rules, and truths come in neatly labeled, black-and-white packages. She may find it hard to understand that rules have exceptions, or that sometimes innocent people get hurt. Happily, you can expect more flexibility in thinking as the child enters the junior-high or middle-school years.

Opening to the world beyond the family. In addition to being active intellectually, your school-age child is entering social circles outside the home. Friends are important; so is being popular at school and not being different from the other children. Having the right clothes and the right toys may become consuming passions as your child reaches the upper elementary years. There may be some attempts at deeper friendships with children of the opposite sex—and there may be some real sexual curiosity. Your child is gearing up for adolescence, and this may happen much sooner than you'd like it to.

Caring for the School-Age Child

High-octane years. One thing in particular will impress you about your school-age child: that high energy level. Your job is to channel that energy into safe directions. Games, sports, and dance are all good ways.

Balancing the limits with the need to explore. In this area, some parents carry limits too far. In the name of love and concern for safety, it's easy to shelter and overprotect your child with chronic illness. Placing unreasonable restrictions on his activity does not help him.

Again, you will need to strike a balance between safety and your child's natural impulse toward exploration and constant activity. Give him as much independence as you possibly can. Also, work through any anxiety you may experience about your child's activity. Excessive worry on your part is contagious: Your child will sense it not only from your words but from your gestures and tone of voice as well.

Building good health habits. Regular visits to the dentist and doctor are important during the early school years. It's common for many children this age to start having problems with cavities. (This is true for children without chronic illness also.) So, dental care is even more important now than it was during the preschool years. Good vision and good hearing are important to success at school, so ask to have these checked at your health care visits.

Even though your school-age child is so active, her food intake may seem greatly slowed. When your child does eat, make sure you've provided varied and nutritious food. Put some energy, too, into providing healthful snacks—food your child can eat on the run. It's all too tempting for children this age to rely on potato chips, candy bars, and soda pop for quick shots of energy. Plan your grocery selections carefully: Making wise food choices sets a good example.

Be sure to check with your child's physician about restrictions on exercise or physical activity. Keep asking questions until you get clear, workable guidelines on what your child can or can't do. This is especially important for the more rough-and-tumble, competitive sports, like hockey or football.

Within those guidelines, though, allow as much physical activity for your child as possible. Relax your natural urge to shelter him, and remind yourself that children don't "break" easily. In fact, their resilience will surprise you. All those cuts, bruises, and scrapes from normal play will quickly fade away.

Your child and friends. During the school years, chronic illness will become a large part of your child's identity. One area in particular is affected: friendships. You can help your child build a circle of relationships by opening your home to your child's friends. Encourage friendships and promote group activities your child enjoys.

Your child as your friend. The possibility of genuine friendship with your child opens to you with the increased communication abilities your child acquires during these years. Now you can talk about more things than you ever talked about before. You might have extended discussions about friends, relatives, brothers, sisters, and events from the evening news.

Keep in mind, though, that your child still can't understand all the details about his chronic illness. You will have to "translate" the basic facts into terms he can understand. Your child wants a working vocabulary to describe her condition to other children and adults, but save the detailed medical whys and hows for a later age. And, avoid "dumping" your concerns and worries on your child. To work through those feelings, you will need a sympathetic listener from your own peer group.

Particularly in this area of emotions you are the key role model for your child. If you hesitate to share what you're thinking, or if you keep to yourself when things are bothering you, your child may conclude that this is the best way to cope with stress.

As you encourage your child to talk more, remember that faltering expression, repetition, and occasional stuttering are common in children this age. For most children, this reflects the effort to master language and logical thinking; it seldom indicates a disability. While these may slow down his speech, they will seldom inhibit him.

Most often your job will be to make sure every one in the family gets a chance to talk, and to do this without squelching your child's passion for conversation. If your child interrupts others frequently, explain calmly that you're glad to hear what she has to say, but that someone else needs a turn right now.

"Why am I different?" By the time they start school, most children with a chronic illness are aware that they're "different" from other children. This is a delicate and sensitive issue for you to handle. We've found that discussing two things in particular often helps:

• Health is a concern for everyone today—adults as well as children. Talk about chronic conditions such as low-back pain, allergies, and high blood pressure that affect so many adults. Mention diabetes, asthma, seizure disorders along with other conditions like obesity, short-stature, and crooked teeth that affect children in her age group. In short, emphasize that your child is not alone.

• Differences are good. Your child is unique, has a personality unlike anyone else's, and has a totally individual way of seeing the world. His special abilities mean that he'll make a contribution to the world that no one else can. This is true despite chronic illness.

You may want to be prepared to tell your child about an accomplished adult who has contributed much to the world while struggling with the same chronic illness. Promoting this kind of positive role model can have many benefits and is not at all the same as making comparisons as discussed in earlier chapters.

During the school years your child should become very involved in his own care. He can perhaps administer his own medications and look after his own special needs. The parent should provide the structure to help the child remember what should happen each day.

The child should also be helping with meal planning, grocery shopping, cooking, and other household tasks—particularly those related to his care. He needs to be encouraged to plan ahead for special events—birthday parties, Halloween, Valentine's Day. You often have to ask such questions as "What will you eat?" "When will you take your medications?" and "Will a late bedtime affect your schedule?" The child should come up with answers and a plan. When the plan works, be sure to praise your child and use that success as a positive experience for the next special day.

Allow overnights at friends' homes, or grandma's, or with the scout troop. Work with your child in planning what needs to be packed and what needs to be communicated to the adults in charge.

It's often a good idea to let your child help decide who she should tell about her chronic illness. True, a core of important people need to know: teachers, close friends, coaches, and the adults in homes your child visits frequently. Still, the facts don't have to be "broadcast" to the general public. Don't confuse your own needs with your child's in this area. Trust your child's growing instincts about who should and should not know. Don't betray these wishes.

Your child's wider world. It may be difficult for some parents to accept their child's widening circle of relationships. It's at this age that you need to start letting go of your child. Indeed, this is a skill you'll need even more in the adolescent and early adult years. It's best to begin now.

Now is also the time to make sure your child has information about the consequences of tobacco, drug, and alcohol use. Statistics show that most children are exposed to these risks around age 10—sometimes even earlier. Information about birth control is often appropriate before the child reaches the adolescent years. Think and plan now for how you want your child to receive this information.

Be prepared also for another important consequence of your child's expanded world. In visiting other homes and getting to know friends at school, your child will observe that "other families do things differently." Now your child starts to notice every kind of difference between people—differences in values, religious beliefs, manners, family traditions, styles of discipline, income, and much more.

Though this can be awkward for both you and your child, keep things in perspective. Seeing alternative ways of thinking, believing, and acting is actually the heart of education. When your child asks questions about these alternatives, don't get defensive. She is just trying to straighten things out mentally, to sort through the vast diversity in the world and put everything into a tentative order. Remember, too, that you are still the strongest and most important influence on your child.

Fostering competence. One of the school-age child's greatest needs is to feel competent. This motive underlies play, school experiences, work around the house—in fact, just about everything your child does. You can help by offering lots of encouragement and paying more attention to the process rather than to the results.

For example: Your child is helping you wash the dishes. In this case, praise your child for offering to help and compliment him on the plates that are really clean. Don't make a big deal out of the plate that still has a small stain. Also, remember that your attitude toward household chores rubs off on your child. If you find something tedious and boring, chances are your child will adopt that view, too.

Building competency becomes a little more complicated when it comes to performance at school. You should decide early on what role you'll play in academics: Will you remind your child to do homework? How often? Will you help with homework? How much? Will you attend school events regularly and participate in parent-teacher conferences?

Doing well in school. Naturally, you want your child to do well at school. Keep track of your child's progress in different subjects. Get extra help—tutoring, extra classes, summer school—when it's called for. But keep the larger picture in mind, too.

At this age, it's not so important that your child excel at memorizing a large body of facts. What's more crucial is that your child master the basics of words and numbers—and that she retain an enthusiasm for learning. This is far more important than straight A's on report cards.

So, round out your child's learning experiences by providing "nonacademic" education. Go to concerts. Visit the library. Conduct spontaneous tours of your city. Let your child see your office at work, and, if possible, let her spend some time there to see you in action. Do your best to discuss things you experience together.

You'll still be tested. You're likely to be puzzled by one aspect of your child's behavior during these years: He'll test your limits—frequently and forcefully. That may appear in bouts of sarcasm, talking back, fighting, and name calling. Even more disturbing to you will be to occasionally catch your child lying or stealing. Yet, she'll often be her own harshest critic. And underlying anti-social behavior can be fear and anger about living with a chronic illness.

How should you respond? For one thing, keep track of your child's behavior. Continue to set clear limits. Calmly, without shaming your child, ask why he acted the way he did. But watch how you "come down" on your child. It's not always necessary to impose strict punishment. Sometimes it's enough to point out that rules have been broken and that you're disappointed. You can also help your child sort through the consequences of her action, asking him to consider how he's hurt other people and disappointed them.

Reader's Digest recently published the following list of "Ten Ways to Turn Out Terrific Kids" by Ray Maloney, which summarizes much of what we've been discussing about dealing with the school-age child. We present this for your consideration:

1. Love them.
2. Build their self-esteem.
3. Challenge them.
4. Listen to them.
5. Expect respect.
6. Limit them.
7. Make God a part of their lives.
8. Develop a love of learning.
9. Help them to be community-minded.
10. Let them go.

Chapter Ten

THE ADOLESCENT

I would that there were no age between ten
and three and twenty; or that youth would
sleep out the rest . . .
William Shakespeare, *Winter's Tale*

How the adolescent grows. William Shakespeare's words confirm to us that the challenges adults face when living with adolescents are far from new. Physical, intellectual, and emotional changes occur in teenagers at an explosive rate—changes that confound, fascinate, and exasperate teenagers and parents alike.

Physical changes include the appearance of the "secondary sex characteristics." For girls, this physical maturation begins around ages 10 to 12. Increased growth of body hair, weight gain, enlarging of breasts, the first menstrual cycle—all are part of this growth process.

Boys may begin this stage as much as 2 to 4 years later than girls. Your son can be expected to gain rapidly in height and weight; you'll see more hair appear on his body; you'll notice the beginnings of a beard and hear the cracklings of a voice that's beginning to deepen in pitch.

Heightened interest in the opposite sex accompanies these physical changes in both boys and girls.

Sex and sexuality. It is important to understand and remember that most often an interest and attraction to the opposite sex begins before these physical changes can be observed. Girls often have "good feelings" about boys before they start to wear a bra or have a menstrual cycle.

Their interest in sexuality finds expression in many ways and, as we said, often begins before parents are ready to deal with it.

Actually, sexuality is the key word here for both boys and girls. By this we mean something beyond interest in genital sex. In reality, sexuality refers to everything that makes women and men different from each other. This includes not only physical characteristics, but behaviors, attitudes, and even values. Ideas about what women and men are supposed to be affect everything: choice of clothing; choice of dating partners—or whether or not to date at all—and eventually, a choice of career.

Body and emotions on a roller coaster. All this physical development requires fuel—energy from food and sleep. Teenagers will eat more (though boys may not experience the weight gain you'd expect from the increases you observe in food intake). While at times your teenage boy or girl seems to move with the speed of a launched missile, expect a "crash"—marathon naps on Sunday afternoon, Saturdays where you're lucky to see your child rise before noon.

The ups and downs of physical activity are matched by emotional peaks and valleys. From secret suicidal fantasies to the euphoria of the first "true" love; from smouldering, moody silence to manic enthusiasm—you'll see it all. You may be frightened by these mood swings and wonder if your adolescent is "normal." In almost all cases, there is no need for worry. Though your child may be shedding tears one minute and screaming at you an hour later, this is all part of the agenda in adolescent years.

Remember, this is due in part to the rampaging hormones that are changing your teenager's body. Fear is a big factor—fear about being accepted by friends and by members of the opposite sex; fear about sexual incompetence; and fear about competence in school. Some of these fears may still be vivid memories from your own teenage years.

The adolescent personality. You can expect passionate criticism of the "system," of authority, of government, of school, of industry—and of you—from your adolescent child. In fact, your teenager may compare you to other parents or measure you against some vision of the "ideal" parent. You can expect to come up short.

Taking on the world and taming the heart. For the adolescent, all subjects are fair game for argument: sex, music, religion, philosophy, politics. This is a time for your teenager to contradict every lesson you've tried to teach. If you like Brahms, expect to see a stash of "punk" rock tapes in your teen's bedroom, recorded by groups that look like extraterrestrials. If you're faithful churchgoers, don't be surprised to hear your child chant slogans of atheism or quote from the Buddhist scriptures.

The adolescent years are years of introspection, as well as reaction. For some children, this means getting in touch with emotions. Writing long journal entries dense with feeling; getting lost in the poetry of Walt Whitman and Emily Dickinson, your youngster will be defining her passions during these years. But, these years will also be self-centered years, as they need to be. Your teenager is trying to figure himself out, and that's the largest task any of us faces.

All of this, however, may frighten you. Take heart and remember to take the long view. Your teenager needs to try on new ideas and behaviors during this time. He's maturing and preparing for his next rite of passage into adulthood and total independence. To reach that stage, she must separate from you, and going to extremes is just part of the search for finding the middle road. Exploration is a vital part of the process.

Remember, too, as you try to sort out this bewildering array of ideas and behaviors that many of these ideas and roles your teenager is flirting with will be just that—flirtations. It remains true that one day your child will be more like you than you ever dreamed possible.

Setting limits without preaching. So, giving your adolescent some latitude to experiment is a key part of your parental role. Within limits, you will need to accept much of this experimentation. It's still crucial, however, that you set limits. Trying on new ideas is one thing; taking dangerous risks is quite another.

Almost daily, our older teens must make decisions about sexual contact, alcohol use, drugs, peer pressure, how to spend money, or how to handle the new freedom that comes with a driver's license. Understandably, this is all too much for some children. Sadly, the rising incidence of teenage suicides substantiates this.

Do you remember how you felt during these years? For many parents, memories of adolescence are still vivid and potent. As we heard one parent say, "Thank God I never have to be 15 again." Remembering some of your own conflicts and experiences may give you some insight into what your child is going through.

So, now is the time for you to talk to your adolescent about where you stand on all these issues. Doing this without preaching and acknowledging every response your teenager makes increases your chances of getting a better response from your child. This does not mean agreeing with everything your child says, nor does it mean silencing your own opinions. Rather, state your opinions clearly and tell your child what worked for you.

Set limits. If drinking alcohol is not part of your lifestyle and you don't want alcohol in your house, say so. If your teenager has to be home by 11:00 PM on Saturday night, stick to that rule. Make the consequences of violating the limits clear. Then enforce those consequences and **do this consistently.**

Caring for Your Adolescent

Promoting your adolescent's physical health. Raging hormones, new and intense sexual urges, rapid physical maturity, mood swings—it reads like a prescription for turbulence and it typifies these teenage years. All this rapid change has some pretty visible—and occasionally upsetting—consequences. Talking about them could bring welcome relief to your teenager. At times, she may recoil at the idea of talking with you about anything. But it's important to try. If nothing else, offering to talk sends out a message reminding your teenager that you care.

Remember that mood swings are usually sudden and unpredictable, and entirely normal. Still, you should try to talk things out whenever possible, trying to define the underlying causes and keeping the lines of communication open.

Self-care. By now your child should have the primary responsibility for managing his chronic illness. The adolescent should be making choices about diet, exercise, levels of physical activity, amount of sleep, and the like. Further, your adolescent deserves all the information about her illness that you can provide. Now is the time to share all that you know—and to express some of your concerns and fears as well.

In short, you'll have to start letting go—with love and limits. By the time your child finishes adolescence, your influence in molding his values is probably minimal. This does not, however, mean that your job as parent is finished. But, it does mean that the nature of the parenting task is shifting.

You no longer have to carefully set detailed limits nor do you constantly have to monitor behavior. Instead, your relationship with your young adult becomes more like that of an equal–you can really become friends. And, as with any friendship, that relationship can be expected to have both tender and turbulent moments.

During these years it's important to remind your teenager that increased medication dosages do not necessarily mean a worsening in the condition. With diabetes, for example, increased insulin levels are needed because of increasing body size and hormonal activity. With your health care team, monitor medication dosages during these years and discuss what's happening with your adolescent.

Adolescent education. You may feel frustrated during these years when you try to help your teenager with homework. Calculus, computer science, contemporary American literature, physics, chemistry–it might all seem out of your current grasp. Perhaps much of it is new to you. Right now your teenager doesn't expect you to understand it all, but you can still display an active interest in what your child is doing at school by talking with her about it. Perhaps he can now begin teaching something new to you and you can encourage him by expressing your enthusiasm.

Adolescence and the terrible temptations. As we said, experimentation during the teen years is part of the program. Trying new things, testing new territories, and learning about self-imposed limits is vital to self-definition. One area commonly explored during adolescence is the use of alcohol. Unfortunately, alcohol use is becoming increasingly popular among adolescents and many youngsters feel pressured to try it. A recent study revealed that as many as 1 in every 7 high school seniors has used alcohol to the point of inebriation on a weekly basis.[1]

Alcohol poses special risks to youngsters with chronic diseases. In diabetes, for example, alcohol can lower blood sugar and an insulin reaction can be mistaken for drunkenness. In everyone, alcohol can impair judgement and make people careless–causing them to abandon their plans for self-care.

It is naive for adults to think their teenagers will never drink. If a teenager, knowing the risks, still decides to drink, he should know the guidelines for using alcohol as it relates to his chronic illness.

· ·

1. Minnesota Adolescent Health Survey; 1986–87 survey of 36,000 public school students.

You may want to reproduce this list and give it to your child when the time of alcohol experimentation arrives:

- Know the detrimental effects of alcohol. It's safest not to drink, but if you feel you must, take precautions.
- Be sure you have your medical ID on you—either wear a bracelet or necklace. Remember that police are not allowed to go into your wallet without your permission, so your medical ID must be easily visible in the event of mishap.
- Limit yourself to two alcoholic drinks.
- Make sure at least one friend at the party knows that you have a chronic illness and knows what the warning signs are of adverse reactions.
- Drink slowly. Sometimes one drink will satisfy that need to feel a part of the crowd.
- If possible, mix or pour your own drink so you know exactly what it contains.
- The less alcohol in the drink the better. Light wines or light beers tend to have reasonably low alcohol contents. Alcohol can be diluted by mixing it with diet soda or club soda.
- Alcohol can stimulate the appetite. Try to avoid binging on tempting party snacks, particularly if you have diabetes.
- Do not substitute alcohol for meals or snacks and do not drink on an empty stomach.
- Drinking and driving do not mix. Why not be the "designated driver" who doesn't drink but who gets others home safely?
- Ask your doctor about how other drugs (cold medications, cough syrups, epilepsy or asthma medications, antihistamines, or whatever you may be taking) will interact with alcohol. Get the best information you can before you choose to drink.

Tobacco. Despite widely publicized health risks many adolescents smoke tobacco. In fact, the Minnesota Survey[2] showed an incidence of nearly 16 percent of teenagers who smoke cigarettes daily. This occurs despite the fact that each year, an estimated 80,000 deaths from lung cancer and 225,000 deaths from cardiovascular disease (heart attack, stroke, atherosclerosis) are linked with smoking.

Combining smoking with a chronic illness results in a much greater risk than smoking alone. Still, many teens will decide to smoke. Parents

. . . .

2. Ibid.

should make the facts about smoking available and should refrain from smoking themselves in an effort to help the child resist.

Crack, marijuana, and other drugs. Teenagers are often attracted to illegal drugs because of peer pressure, an erroneous belief that these drugs are safe, and the notion that "doing drugs" is a sign of maturity. It is often difficult for parents to dissuade their youngsters from experimenting with drugs without sounding judgemental.

Many schools now have drug awareness and dependency prevention programs that can help. Find out about these and encourage your child to participate in them. Try to have calm discussions about drugs, discussions where you listen to your child's feelings and acknowledge the youngster's pressures and curiosity. You can tell your child that you prefer he not experiment but remind him that you trust his judgement in making decisions for himself. Urge her to take precautions if she must experiment.

Sex and birth control. Sexually active youth need information about contraceptives, and a sexually active youth with a chronic illness may need additional help in choosing a safe, effective method. While this topic may be unsettling for parents, it, nonetheless, needs to be realistically considered. The facts are that young people—really "children"—are physiologically capable of conceiving a child by the age of 12.

When a parent learns or suspects the child is sexually active, the question is usually not "Should my daughter be sexually active or not?" . . . it is more likely to be "Is it better that she use a contraceptive than run the risk of becoming pregnant?" The choice to be sexually active is another form of exploration and experimentation that many adolescents undertake. Accurate information about pregnancy and contraceptive methods, how to obtain them and how to use them, needs to be supplied. You can play a major role in how your child receives this information by talking about it in a straightforward way and offering to help get any specific questions answered by a health professional.

AIDS education. Acquired immune deficiency syndrome, or AIDS, is a major public health issue today. Sexually transmitted diseases are an ever present medical problem. All are preventable, but drug use, sexual abuse, and carelessness in sexual activity contribute to the problem.

Sexual health and responsibility needs to be addressed and addressed early. If you, as parents, are not knowledgeable or comfortable in the role of sex educator, talk to your health care team and see that some other competent adolescent-friendly professional does the job.

Driving. Getting a driver's license is a major milestone in your young adult's life. The special risks associated with driving may mean special restrictions when your youngster has a chronic illness. You will need to understand the laws of your state regulating licensing to know if a doctor's clearance is needed, or what rules and reporting procedures relate to your child's particular chronic illness.

All states have regulations of one kind or another for drivers with epilepsy or insulin-requiring diabetes, for example, but the regulations vary widely. In some states, a person with epilepsy must be free of seizures for between six and twelve months before he can obtain a driver's license. The trend is toward shorter seizure-free periods in other states. However, most states still require that medical reports be submitted from time to time so the driver's chronic condition can be monitored. It is, therefore, important that you check with your state's department of public safety or transportation before approaching the question of driving so that your adolescent can know all the facts.

Keeping in touch with your teenager. Despite your teen-age child's growing mental powers, don't expect cool rationality from him all the time. Often the powers of reason don't mesh well with the volatile emotions of adolescence. Try to understand this. When your teenager makes excuses about skipping a medical appointment or missing a dose of medication, think about how you, too, rationalize for neglecting exercise or eating two pieces of pie when one was more than enough. Rationalizing doesn't excuse behavior, but it can give you a common ground for discussing the problem.

One of the hardest things for many parents to deal with is the seeming self-centeredness of adolescents. Your daughter seems to be constantly concerned with her appearance, her problems, her moods, her opinions, her wardrobe. To escape your scrutiny and criticism, she may withdraw verbally and emotionally from you. When you get the silent treatment, when your teenager is sullen and withdrawn, you may feel locked out.

At the same time, your teenager's heart seems to bleed for everyone. Now he's angered by social injustice; he disputes your politics and religion; he thinks you are complacent and self-centered. It's easy to get defensive under this kind of attack.

Listening is your lifeline. Most of the time, all this is normal. More than ever, you will fail if you try to demand intimacy or conformity from your adolescent. You can't command him to talk or force him to tell you what's behind his angry looks or occasional tears, nor can you insist that he agree with you. However, you can send out a lifeline.

That lifeline is listening – active, interested, careful, nonjudgemental listening. These are great years during which to practice your skills as a listener. When your teenager *does* talk, seize the moment. Make it count.

It's okay, however, to let the teenager who talks incessantly know that you have limits. You might say, "I'm exhausted and it's midnight, but I want to hear what you have to say. Let's talk at 4 o'clock tomorrow. I'll wait for you after school."

The following are suggestions for better listening:

• Suspend judgement. Many parents find it helpful to say nothing but a sympathetic "Ummmm," or "Ahhh," at first. Professional counselors do this frequently.

• Save your criticism for later and try not to jump to conclusions. Give your child a fair hearing. At the beginning, let her do the talking.

• Be sensitive to your body language and tone of voice. When your adolescent talks, what's your facial expression like? Are your frowning? Smiling? Receptive and concerned? Or just blank? Are your muscles relaxed or tense?

You can absorb ideas much faster than most speakers can express them, so take advantage of that extra mental speed to note your body signals. Avoid signals that turn your teenager off – crossed arms, leaning away, no eye contact, forbidding facial expressions.

• If nothing else, keep in mind one point: We spend far too much time criticizing other people's viewpoints – and too little trying to understand what they really meant in the first place.

If you're in the throes of an argument with your teenager, take a mental pause. Take a deep breath and try to relax your muscles. Then, before you respond to what your teenager is saying, take a minute to summarize what he said. Ask him if you stated his case accurately. Only when you have done this should you state your side of the issue. Of course, you have the right to ask your teenager to give you the same treatment.

- Recognize your emotional triggers. All of us have strong attachments to certain ideas and opinions. When someone challenges them, we feel personally attacked. Birth control, abortion, welfare, crime, arms control, religion—these and hundreds of other topics commonly arouse emotional debate.

Most of us are simply not willing to yield ground on our cherished opinions. It's almost as if we defy people to change our minds! This attitude is a hindrance to good listening. Try to recognize it in yourself.

Dr. Lyman Steil, former speech professor and now a corporate trainer, calls this the "valued moment of listening." According to this idea, you never know when an important fact or hidden feeling will emerge during a conversation. Rather, you must be prepared for it at any moment.

Sarcasm is destructive. Your teenager is especially sensitive about her looks, ideas, choice of friends, choice of music, and in a score of other areas. Many parents try to lighten things up by joking about these things. However, rarely does this approach yield an appreciative response. A sense of humor during these years may not be one of your child's strongest characteristics. It is best to tread lightly with teasing—if you decide to tease at all. Sarcasm, in particular, should be avoided. The word "sarcasm" originally meant "to tear the flesh." Think of this definition when you're tempted to be sarcastic.

Don't win arguments, win friends. Above all, it helps many parents to just loosen up a bit. Do you have to be right all the time? Do you have to win every battle? Of course not. Be willing to entertain new ideas. (This doesn't mean accepting them right away.) You might learn something new.

Be willing to admit that times are different today, that it's okay for your child to disagree with you on a wide range of issues. In fact, you can disagree on many issues and still love each other. After all, would you demand total agreement with your viewpoint from any of your closest friends?

The world is more complex today than it was even one generation ago, and all indications point to increasing complexity in the future. Your child has many choices to make—perhaps far more than you did at his age. By these choices we mean choices in career, in sex roles, in religious affiliation, in books to read, in movies to view, in attendance at various cultural events. With some thought, you can easily expand this list.

Does this expanded choice call for a permissive, "anything goes" attitude toward your teenager? Not at all. Yes, you have to listen, admit mistakes, and show some flexibility. But yes, you still have the right and the responsibility to set limits. Almost all of these limits should relate to concrete behaviors—not to ideas or opinions.

Define what areas you'll negotiate on. (And we hope you'll define many of them.) Decide what areas are non-negotiable, and don't budge. Keep your "edicts." There should not be too many of these. To keep perspective, remember the experience of one family we know. The parents refused to let their teenaged son drive the family car to a school dance unless he got his hair cut. Adolescent pride wouldn't let him lose this battle, so he hitched a ride. His driver was drunk, and there was an accident in which he was killed. In their sorrow, these parents realized immediately that the length of their son's hair did not warrant such an inflexible rule.

Too often, the most blistering arguments with teenagers result not because there are limits, but because those limits were not clear in the first place. To guard against this, talk over your answers to these questions when tempers are cool:

• What choices will you give your teenager about relationships with the opposite sex? When is it okay to start dating? How late can your child stay out? What activities are acceptable? What do you say about contraceptives and birth control? How can you help your child learn about intimate relationships and expressing sexuality without intercourse?

• How closely will you monitor your child's chronic illness and self-care? And what choices will you leave totally up to your teenager's discretion? How far do you trust your child to manage medication, schedule medical appointments, and regulate exercise and sleep?

• What's your role in encouraging good performance at school? Do you have expectations for the amount of time to be spent on homework? How about the amount of time your child can spend on sports, music, and other "non-academic" subjects?

• How much access will your teenager have to the family car? Who pays for added costs, such as gas and insurance?

• How many hours each week can your teenager work outside the home? What happens to the wages earned? Who balances the checkbook and decides what should be saved?

• What family traditions do you expect your child to participate in? These include visits to relatives, family vacations, family meetings, and the ways you observe holidays.

• If your family's religious life is important to you, how do you want your child to take part? Do you want your adolescent to attend church or synagogue regularly? Are there other religious practices that you want everyone in the family to observe?

• How much will you "let go" of the care for your child's chronic illness? Do you feel guilty about turning the tasks of daily care back to your child? Can you trust your teenager's judgement and ability to evaluate the consequences of his actions?

This last point reminds us of something essential in adolescence. Perhaps more than anything else, this is the time for your child to examine every viewpoint and to question everything. To see this openness and receptivity develop in your child is really something wonderful, something to celebrate, even when the results raise your defenses.

What you do still matters. Remember that your adolescent is trying out various identities during these years—almost as casually as she changes her clothes. Over time, the range of choices will narrow. And, some enduring values will emerge. Many of the self-defeating behaviors will fall away.

In the transformation of your youngster from hesitant, diffident child to fully functioning adult, you still play the major role. Your actions have a more enduring impact on your child than those of teachers, coaches, peers, or anyone else.

Your chances for success are greater if you stay open—if you're willing to re-examine your values, if you're willing to listen to your child, if you're willing to question things again. In the end, living with an adolescent can make you feel more alive and aware. But you must remain the parent. You never stop being a parent. Your youngsters will make mistakes, but don't judge them too harshly. You were once a teenager, too.

Chapter Eleven
. . . .
THE EVERYDAY CONCERNS

There is more to parenting, obviously, than just mastering the information about growth and development, and these seemingly little things that come up everyday can make or break you. Decisions you must make about discipline, sibling rivalry, advice from well-meaning relatives, eating behaviors, and contact with the world of health care have a great impact on your family. This chapter will offer some practical suggestions for dealing with these everyday concerns.

Before we get started, however, we urge you to find solace in the fact that many parents who are raising children with chronic illnesses are doing an excellent job of it. Some days are better than others, but over-all these families are very successful, as measured—not by the best laboratory results but—by their ability to function as a family with happy, "healthy" children.

Secrets of Success: Families Who Live Well with Chronic Illness

Fortunately, we've been able to work with families who do foster healthy independence in their children with chronic illnesses. Families who do a good job coping with chronic illness have some particular attitudes in common, as illustrated by the following comments:

• "We strive for a constructive balance in our relationships".

In our "model" families, parents and children find a middle ground where everyone's rights are respected. Parents set limits that are clear and fair, and those limits are enforced consistently. Children usually don't feel the limits are either too strict or too lax. What's more, parents strive to let go of their child's chronic illness whenever it's safe to do so. This means letting the child take over responsibility for daily care. Parents neither overprotect nor neglect the child.

• "Life works best when we see that our child with chronic illness is, above all, a child—not a package of symptoms."

Never, for example, refer to a child with diabetes as a "diabetic" or the child with seizure disorder as an epileptic. Using such terms implies that the person and the disease are the same. This use of language fogs our thinking and ultimately controls how we treat the child. A person with asthma is—first and foremost—a person. The same should be said where diabetes, epilepsy, or any other chronic condition is involved.

• "Chronic illness does not have to rule our family."

Life is much more than illness. Work, play, friends, sexuality, solitude, spirituality, education—all these things ask for attention. There are parents' needs to consider. For many of us, there are also brothers and sisters to cherish. We put a lot of energy into helping our child with chronic illness, and at times this must take precedence. But, this issue is still not the main thing in our lives.

• "We love all our children without conditions."

This must be true whether or not chronic illness is a factor. What do we mean by that term "unconditional love?" Here are some examples:

• If our children get high grades from kindergarten through college, that's fine. But we'll love them even if they don't set the academic world on fire.

• If our children become world-class athletes and compete in the Olympics, that's great. But we'll love them even if they don't know a volleyball from a football, or if they strike out every time they're at bat.

• Perhaps our children will strive to become concert pianists, surgeons, corporate executives, or university presidents. If that's what they choose—fine. But we'll still love them if they become cabinet makers or garbage collectors. When it comes to choosing a vocation, we only hope our children follow their hearts and their enthusiasms.

Our job as parents is to loosen the reigns as we go along. Our goal is to raise children who are responsible for their own lives. We want to produce adults who make choices, judge, and take the consequences of their actions, and adults who are self-confident enough to take some risks.

When our children are young, we nurture and protect them. But there are higher aims in life than safety. Being a parent means gradually turning over responsibility to our children—as soon as they can safely handle it. So, as our children grow, we begin to let go.

Asserting Discipline while Communicating Love

It's true that chronic illness changes the whole texture of your family life. It also influences your style as mentor—that is, how you set limits and discipline your children. In the following pages we offer some guidelines for handling this role.

Remember, there's room for individual differences. To illustrate, we offer an example about grasping at simple rules for parenting:

You read a great book about how to discipline children and eagerly share your enthusiasm with every parent in the neighborhood. Perhaps the idea that excites you is the "I'm OK, You're OK" philosophy. Maybe it's using "logical consequences" or "natural consequences." Perhaps it's a technique no one's heard of before. In any case, you decide that this one approach is the key to being a successful parent.

To prove your point, you even make a pact with one other family: "I'd like to try a technique from this book. How about if you try it, too? That way we can support each other." Everyone agrees to follow the same recipe, with visions of the ideal child already forming in their minds.

You check in with the other family two months later. Things are going well for them. Family arguments are almost a thing of the past. Their children never fight with each other, it seems. Dinner time has been transformed from a battle ground to a mutual support session.

Meanwhile, not much has changed for the better at your house. In fact, things may have gotten a little worse. What happened?

Basically, the point is that there are no sure-fire guides or hard and fast methods that will always work in the complex challenge of raising a child. You could memorize what other parents say and do, duplicating their every gesture and word. Will you get the same results as they do? Of course not.

Why? Because you're different from other parents. Your children are different from their children. When you apply a particular technique, you modify it. The technique changes as it becomes your own, as you add your tone and style. In the end, what worked for someone else may not work for you. Being a parent means you may have to abandon some of your cherished beliefs—especially when they fail in everyday life.

When appropriate, the limits you set for children should also apply to you. Can you really limit your child to two hours of TV per week when you stare at the tube for four hours each night? Or can you forbid desserts when your children see you consistently eating gourmet ice cream as your late-night snack? And does it make sense to insist your children attend church school when you sleep until noon every Sunday? To be credible, you should set limits that really reflect your own values—and your own behavior.

Above all, try to be clear, consistent, and fair. One of our main tasks as mentors is to do a good job setting limits. In essence, this means saying three things to our children:

1. There are certain things you can't do while you live with us. We make these rules to protect others as well as you. We want you to know exactly what these things are. If we fail to make ourselves clear about this, then we can't expect you to behave well.

2. We'll try to be consistent. If we give you rules today, you can be sure the same rules will apply tomorrow—and for as long as the rules are needed.

3. We'll do our best to make sure these limits are balanced. We don't want to be too strict. We also don't want to be too lenient.

Some parents impose more rules than their children can possibly remember. Others impose no rules at all—or ignore whatever rules they do impose. In either case, the child can feel confused or insecure.

At times when children are misbehaving, there is the ever-present fear of the loss of self-control. When our frustrations seem to overpower us, we become afraid of what we may say and do. If this happens to you, take a deep breath, relax, and remember: This happens to everyone. Even to those who are not trying to raise children.

The important thing is to be aware of this tendency in yourself. If you sense it's getting the best of you, leave the room, count to 10, go for a short walk – anything to regain your perspective. But don't discipline your children at that moment. If you do try to deal with your children now, you'll only communicate rage – not limits.

Don't expect to succeed all the time. Despite all your efforts, you will blow it sometimes. You'll contradict yourself or get angry with your child simply because you've had a terrible day at work. You'll say something that hurts your child. You'll fail to say "I love you" when it matters the most. You'll do all these things and probably lots more, just as we all do.

You are not God – and no one expects you to be. When it comes to raising children, it's the broad patterns in your behavior that count, not the isolated incidents. It's the perspective of a lifetime that matters – not the argument you had last night.

Ask yourself: Does my child have a basic trust in me? Does she know that whatever happens, I care? If you can honestly say yes to these questions, then you are succeeding as a parent.

See the difference between punishment and discipline. By punishment we mean temporarily taking away something your child values or introducing something your child dislikes. Common examples are spanking, suspending an allowance, taking away TV time, or forbidding your child to see certain friends.

Many parents talk only about these kinds of actions when they think about discipline. However, there's more to discipline than punishment. If discipline means setting an effective example for your child and turning your child in the right direction, then punishment may not always be needed.

When your child violates a limit you've imposed, ask yourself: Is he really sorry about what he's done? Is she already punishing herself through her own shame and humiliation? If you're convinced this is true, then you may be able to sidestep punishment. Perhaps all you need to do is make sure your child knows he made a mistake.

Tailor your discipline to your child's age. Limits are not static. Instead, they should change as your child changes. That means taking into account not only your child's age, but how she's developing—emotionally, mentally, and physically. In addition to what you've already read in earlier chapters, here are some more suggestions about discipline.

Tips for disciplining young children. To begin with, you can't ask an infant to reason or sort through the consequences of his actions. So other tactics must be employed.

One is controlling the environment. Does your infant seem fascinated with that sack of marbles she found in her older brother's room? Does she always crawl toward that long stairway when she's on the upper level of your house? Both these situations are quite dangerous. The logical response is to move that sack of marbles—along with any other dangerous toys—well out of your child's reach. You can also buy a "baby barrier" or similar device that's made to fit in doorways and at the top of stairways. Or, you can simply lay a chair on its side to securely block off an area.

Another powerful tool is distraction. If your toddler keeps reaching for the ruler on your desk, offer him a soft, cuddly stuffed animal instead. When you distract, it's important to offer an alternative. Never simply grab the offending object out of your child's hands.

One word your child comes to understand around age 1 (sometimes even sooner) is "No." It's better to use this simple syllable when restraining your child than to use scolding or explanation—things your infant really doesn't understand anyway. If anything, you can use a few simple words to explain what's off limits. Most importantly, you should enforce those limits consistently.

At almost any age, a loud "No!" will get your point across. As your child matures, though, you should expand your list of responses.

Rewards. Toddlers and preschoolers respond to rewards. Try to make rewards appropriate to the situation. Keep in mind that hugs and kisses are basic rewards, but occasionally material rewards should also be used. As your child gets older, giving stickers for good behavior or stars or ribbons recognizing successes are effective and reasonable reward techniques. You needn't worry that you're "manipulating" your child. To make this work most effectively, though, choose a reward that's meaningful to your child. Be careful not to reward with food, since this can lead to problems later on.

Closely related to reward is praise and affection. It's crucial to remember that discipline goes beyond looking at what's gone wrong: Even more, discipline is paying attention to what's going well. Make a point to praise your child at least once a day for behavior of which you approve. You don't have to go overboard with this. A simple smile, hug, or words of praise is often all that's needed.

Using time outs. "Timing out" your child—briefly removing him from the scene of the unacceptable behavior—is a popular alternative to spanking. This technique has several advantages. For one, it allows your child to calm down and regain some mental and emotional control. You can also use this time to be alone with your child, gain his full attention, and explain clearly what went wrong. To get the best results from a time out, make it short enough so your child has a chance to "get it right"—that is, to return to the situation and behave correctly.

Tips for disciplining older children. For school-age children and adolescents, you can discipline by pointing out the results of behavior. This is what people mean when they talk about being "aware of the consequences." As many psychologists have pointed out, there are two kinds of consequences: natural and logical.

• Natural consequences flow directly from your child's action: If she fails to brush her teeth, she may develop plaque and cavities. If he walks across the street without looking both ways, he may come into the path of a car. If she eats too much after school, her blood sugar will be high that evening. If he doesn't take his medicine, he will wheeze or have a seizure.

• Logical consequences don't always result directly from your child's actions. Instead, these may be consequences you provide. For example, if your child refuses to eat at dinner, you point out that there will be no snacks available later.

The degree of impact for either type of consequence is usually linked to the amount of time between the action and when the consequence occurs. The more immediate the timing of the consequence, the greater the impact.

At any age—listen. As your child masters language and begins to share thoughts and feelings, you can work to become a good listener. This is an effective technique at any age. Listening helps you with discipline: You'll have a greater chance of getting your point across when your child really listens to what you're saying. And one of the best ways to encourage good listening is to become a good listener yourself.

Besides, when you take the time to listen, you immediately gain two advantages: First, you ask your child to explain her behavior and get a chance to hear what's going on in her mind and heart. Second, you deliver a nonverbal message to the child. If he could put this message into words, it would be something like this: "Mom and dad give me a chance to tell my side of the story. They care enough about me to do that, and they think what I have to say is important."

Most people take the ability to listen for granted, forgetting that good listening is active listening: It takes effort. For some tips on listening, see Chapter 10.

Solving behavior problems. Develop an action plan. This is where you truly need to become a "scientific" parent. When psychologists work with a child with behavioral problems, they start with a neutral, objective approach. First, they observe the troublesome behavior and make notes. They also note what happens before the behavior and what comes after it. Then they look at several ways to respond and choose the one they think will be best for the child.

You can borrow some features of this approach. Here are the steps to follow. You might want to make written notes for each step.

1. State—in one or two sentences—what the problem is. When you do this, focus on what your child is doing, and not on how you're reacting.

For example, "Sarah, our 5-year-old, wants to buy a toy every time we go into a department store. When we refuse to go along with this, she cries, and we usually end up leaving the store." This is a good description of what the child is doing. It isolates the problem and limits it to something you can deal with.

The following is not a good description of the problem:

"It just seems we can never go to the store without everybody getting mad at each other. I get really angry when this happens."

2. Ask what comes before the problem behavior. Is there any event that triggers the behavior that you don't like? Answer these questions:

- Did you set clear limits ahead of time? Does the child know exactly what behavior you dislike?
- Does the behavior take place at a certain time?
- Where is the child when the behavior takes place?
- What are you doing at the time and place?
- What's your condition–physically and emotionally–when the problem behavior occurs? Are you tired, hungry, stressed, in a hurry? How about your child?

3. Note how you follow up on the problem behavior:
- How do you respond to the problem behavior?
- Do you enforce limits consistently? Do you sometimes give in to the behavior or simply ignore it?
- Does everybody who has to deal with this behavior–including your spouse, teacher, day-care provider–respond in the same way?

4. Based on your answers, what do you think is the best alternative?
- Would the behavior stop if everyone disciplined it in the same way?
- What response seems most effective when the behavior occurs?
- Does your child really understand what the problem is? Or, is he deliberately ignoring the limits you set?
- Is the limit that you've set reasonable, fair to your child, and clear?

Let's return to the example introduced earlier–the child who demanded that her parents buy her a toy every time they entered a store. Using the steps outlined above, the parents found out they were treating the situation differently: Father usually ignored the request, letting the child cry; if he was tired, however, he bought a toy simply to make peace and then felt resentment afterwards. On the other hand, Mother always refused the request and left the store with the child.

The parents' solution was simple and successful: First, they decided to shop together for the next couple of months. That way, they could make sure the problem was being handled successfully. Next, they explained to Sarah that she was getting no new toys in the next several visits to the store. They made the limit clear: If she insisted on crying at the store, she would have to leave the store with one parent. And if this happened more than twice, Sarah would not be able to go shopping at all for two weeks.

To sum up: The parents explained the behavior they would not allow. They also made clear the consequence of the troublesome behavior and enforced it consistently. This was enough to handle the problem.

Defusing Battles Between Your Children

Sibling rivalry is the psychologist's term for what happens when your children don't get along. You know the symptoms: Fights. Arguments. Complaints that "He gets all the attention," or "You always treat her differently than me."

This is an issue for nearly all families with more than one child. When one of the children has a chronic illness, underlying tensions come to the surface more quickly. This is only natural: It's easy to give your child with chronic illness more attention than your other children.

This problem may occur no matter how hard you work to avoid it. Certain attitudes on your part, though, can make the situation easier to handle. For the most part, these attitudes can be set in place long before the first sibling rivalry occurs.

You can, however, change your attitudes and treat chronic illness with a more positive perspective. If you succeed at this, you won't think about illness all the time. Ask yourself: Is your child's care routine a burden to you most of the time? Or is it something you can use to sell the whole family on taking health more seriously?

Let's say your son has asthma episodes that are tied to emotional outbursts or stress. Do you resent this because it limits how firm you can be when disciplining him? If you do, you'll communicate this quickly to the entire family—even if you never say it in so many words.

Can you shift perspective and say something like this to your other children?

"John has to watch it so he doesn't get too upset. So, if it seems I go easy on him sometimes, that's why. To help us all, though, I'm asking John to learn what to do when he suddenly gets real mad or sad. He's going to work on relaxing and breathing deeply and talking about feelings instead of hiding them. This would be a good thing for all of us to learn—especially me. Why don't we all work on this together?"

You can make sure your child with chronic illness doesn't get an "illness-based" identity. By this we simply mean letting that child know she's a whole person first; her illness is only one of the important things about her.

How do you do this? By making sure that you talk about things other than illness with this child and by not always talking about the illness first followed by other things. By praising his accomplishments at home and school. By sharing activities—sports, trips to the museum, household chores—where chronic illness can be put aside without being ignored.

You can set aside time for your other children. Loving your children equally is a complicated task, but so much of it boils down to simply paying attention. First, look at the quality of your attention when you're around the children. Are you making full contact with them—looking directly at them, actively listening to what they're saying? Or are you trying to accomplish something else at the same time—such as reading the sports page, painting the garage, or watching the news on TV?

Here the two most important things are to make real contact with each child and give each child private time. First, when you're with any of your children, give your full attention. Be fully present. Second, try to find one special activity to share privately with each child. For one child, that may be playing catch; for another, it may be camping or talking about sports. You can even make an appointment: Block out this time on a calendar in each child's room. Then save that date.

Think about the actual messages your children receive. So much of what we say, feel, and do about our children escapes our notice. Actually, this ties into a trait that most humans share: We tend to judge others by what they do. But, we judge ourselves by what we intend. What we forget is that the intention and the act are not always the same.

For example, one father we know was puzzled when his teenage daughter emotionally withdrew from him. They had always been close, sharing long conversations at the dinner table after the dishes were cleaned up. Suddenly, it seemed to him, those conversations stopped. His daughter would offer to help with the dishes and then simply leave.

The problem was simple. Though the father still felt the same affection for his daughter, he had started making jokes about the music she listened to, comparing it to "the noise of a drill hammer." To him this was a simple off-handed comment—a harmless joke, one that their close relationship could easily bear. In fact, he forgot about ever making jokes about the music she preferred.

His daughter didn't agree. Music was becoming more important to her, and it represented an area that was simply off-limits for teasing.

In this case, neither person could see the problem clearly. To the daughter, it seemed that dad had suddenly become insensitive. To dad, it seemed that his daughter had become moody and secretive. Things eased up when mom pointed out the jokes and how they affected their daughter.

This example points to the best way to understand what unconscious messages you're sending out: Ask for feedback from an independent observer. If such a person isn't available, ask your child directly: "What's creating the tension between us right now?"

We emphasize all this because messages about favoritism—"You like him more than me"—are usually sent in this subtle, unconscious way.

Talk about your children without comparing them. "Your sister was always so good in math; I wonder why it's so hard for you." "Eat everything on your plate; your brother always finishes his dinner without complaining." These comments—innocent as they seem to you—can devastate your child. They can also lead to charges of favoritism.

Try this exercise: For one or two days, keep track of every sentence you speak that compares your children with one another. You don't have to try and change anything at this point; simply make note of your comments. When you've done this, look for a pattern in what you've said. Do you praise one child more than another? Does one child get most of the criticism? How would you feel if these comments were directed at you?

Detailed awareness of what you say is the main thing you need to stop this behavior. If you have trouble tracking comparison statements, ask your partner or your children for their help. Make it clear, from what you say and how you react, that their feedback is important to you.

How to Work Things Out with Grandparents and Other Relatives

As we pointed out earlier, becoming a parent brings you into a new relationship with your own parents and other relatives. The newness of it all is exciting—and often frustrating. You may struggle with an onslaught of free advice, expectations, worry, and overindulgence for your child. And when chronic illness becomes part of the extended family, grandparents may not feel prepared for it.

It doesn't have to be this way. Getting along with grandparents can become easier if you apply the following ideas.

Step into your parents' shoes. As a new parent yourself, you're exhilarated, overwhelmed, exhausted, excited, hopeful, and nervous—all at the same time. If chronic illness later becomes a fact of life for your child, you may go through a period of intense self-doubt, wondering whether you can really handle it all.

At that point, your defenses are up. Any advice from grandparents is bound to feel like criticism. A casual comment, it seems, can call into question your whole approach to raising children.

Watch for this reaction in yourself. If you see it, start to operate with a new idea: What sounds like criticism from grandparents is not an attack. Instead, it could be:

- A question
- An alternative for you to consider
- A suggestion
- Concern for your child, masked as overprotectiveness
- An offer to take over for a time so you can get a break.

You no doubt feel a need to be recognized as a concerned, active parent. You may also be trying to meet a hidden agenda—a rigid set of expectations that you did not choose. In the midst of your struggle, you may forget that your parents are working through this, too. Most of them would do anything for their grandchildren. They may also be trying to meet an impossible expectation.

One grandparent summed up the gist of that expectation in these words:

I've been around a while, and I've learned a lot. I must have wisdom to offer my children when they become parents. I want my children to avoid the mistakes I made. All this is necessary before I can feel I'm being a good grandparent.

Your parents are trying to prove themselves, too. They want you to confirm that their ideas are true and useful. They need you now—as much as you needed them when you were younger.

True, you may disagree with some of their ideas. And at times you may not want their help. But it will be easier to resolve conflict if you can see the larger picture and step into your parents' shoes once in a while. Remember this the next time you're angry with them.

Say thank you. Giving your own parents credit from time to time can lighten your relationship and do wonders for their self-esteem. This can be quite simple; comments such as the following will do nicely:

"I appreciate what you do for Mark. He looks forward to seeing you so much."

"Your help means a lot to me. When you take Chris for a night, it gives me a chance to breathe again."

"It's good to get the perspective of someone who's been through all this before."

Ask for help. You can go even farther: You can occasionally ask for a grandparent's opinion. This may flatter them so much that they'll overlook the other times you ignored their advice! And, when a suggestion does work well, be sure to let them know.

Be on the lookout for wisdom. Don't assume that advice from your parents is outdated fact or simple meddling. Yes, you may get some of this. But if you dismiss everything grandparents say, you may miss some real gems.

So, take what they say and think it over. Sift through it with the same attitude you would bring to a book or magazine article on child raising. Think: "Some of this may not work for me, and some might. But it's worth listening to. I'll give it a chance."

Point out ways for grandparents to help. Many times grandparents want to help but have no idea what to do. This can happen more often if they don't have the facts about your child's chronic illness. They need information about the illness and specific ideas about how to care for your child. You will, in most cases, need to be their teacher, providing this vital information.

At these times, they'll appreciate some direct advice from you. Help them learn the details about your child's care routine. Suggest specific ways they can help: "Can you make sure John gets his medication at noon?" "Please help me remember to get Mary inside for a snack at 3 this afternoon."

Deepen your relationship by delving into your family story. When your child is young, you're bound to hear grandparents look back on your childhood: "I remember when you were your daughter's age. Sometimes you were just as forgetful as she is today." "John has the same musical talent you did. I wish we could have afforded more lessons for you back then."

Now is the time for you to ask leading questions. Get grandparents to talk more about the past. Listen without judging, and make them feel safe enough to open up. When this works, your relationship can enter a softer, more mature phase. They're free to express the doubts and fears they had—to admit the mistakes they made. Finally, they can shed the image of having to be perfect. In this kind of atmosphere, you can open up too and talk about the difficulties you're having.

Loosen up. It's easy to feel that grandparents are undercutting what you're trying to do with your children. You're trying to teach the virtues of saving money and planning for the future; meanwhile, grandfather will buy Sarah any toy she wants. You're worried about your child's weight, and grandmother shows up with two plates of steaming chocolate-chip cookies, laden with butter and sugar. You've married into a new religion; when you're not listening, grandfather is passing on children's books that lay out the "correct" spiritual dogma.

Remembering one fact will help you through these times: Your child will be influenced by many people. You are not the only influence on your children. Throughout their lives, they will learn alternatives to everything you teach. In an age of television, radio, newspaper, talk shows, records, and world travel, this simply has to be.

However, our children are more flexible than we realize. Most of them will do a good job sorting through all this information. After all, didn't you? Children also can handle different "styles" of care without forever changing their personalities.

True, grandparents may overindulge your child when they visit. Still, he'll understand that the rules of the game have changed for only a few hours. Your children will still look to you as the main influence in their lives. And if grandparents spoil your children a little, always commenting on how wonderful your children are, is that such a bad message to hear?

Let grandparents know your limits. Despite what we've just said, you don't have to accept everything your child's grandparents do. It helps if you take the initiative here. Before a conflict arises, talk casually about your basic household rules—especially the rules about caring for your children:

"Joanne can have hypoglycemia, so she needs to snack several times each day. Here's the food we give her."

"This is a bad time of year for pollen and spores. Here is the medicine Chris takes for allergies in the spring."

"If Gary misses a dose of medication, his seizures are worse. When that happens, we ask him to stay inside and rest for the afternoon."

Point out, too, that you're trying to give equal attention to all the children in your family—and not to dote on the child with a chronic illness.

Most grandparents will be happy to abide by the rules. They simply need to be clear on what the limits are.

Feeding the Whole Family Well

Diabetes! My daughter, Arin, was only five when her diabetes was diagnosed. How, my husband and I wondered, would she cope with all the control and responsibility diabetes demands? Many preschoolers learn about the importance of eating a well-balanced diet, but Arin would also have to learn about carbohydrates, proteins, and fats, and the importance of balancing exercise, insulin and food—we were wrong to worry about her learning ability.

By the time she was discharged from the hospital, Arin understood why she had to take insulin. She also knew that diabetes is forever. She knew she would have to balance her insulin, food and exercise, and follow a more rigid schedule than she had before. She knew a lot. Unfortunately, when it came to practicing her knowledge, she surprised us again. Although she had no problem accepting injections or testing, she refused to finish her meals. At home, meals became a hassle; the more we tried to get her to eat, the more she resisted.

Hall and Keltz, "What To Do When Your Child Won't Eat,"
Diabetes Forecast, May/June, 1980.

Balanced nutrition is a prime factor in controlling many chronic conditions such as diabetes. In other cases, eating well can help your child's overall health. The result is more energy to live well with a chronic illness.

It's often with food that chronic illness becomes a family affair. Parents don't really want to juggle two different meal plans—one for the child with chronic illness, another for the rest of the family. Though this is necessary at times, you can still look for ways to balance everyone's needs.

One fact will help you do this: Most often what's good for a child with chronic illness is also good for you. Food is a good example. Often what your health care team prescribes is an ideal for the whole family: less fat, less sugar, lower cholesterol, more whole grains and vegetables, leaner meat and more fruit.

In short, a chronic illness often demands a change in lifestyle, including how you eat. But in many cases you can, in truth, sell this change as a ticket to health for the whole family. Though nutrition is not the only factor in good health, it's an area where you can make a difference right away.

Don't let food be a weapon: feeding finicky eaters. Most parents find they can't force changes in diet. In many cases, a low-profile, gradual change is best.

Mealtimes are frequently occasions for family battles. Sometimes, in fact, it may seem that your child stockpiles all his grievances for the evening meal—just the time you need peace and harmony the most.

Take steps to defuse those battles before they arise:
- Involve your children in preparing meals. Let them mix ingredients, set the table, even plan menus. By involving them up front, you can make them your allies in food preparation.

- Encourage family members to help you prepare meals. Let them see new foods in the making. Young children, especially, will relish this.
- Don't, however, expect your child to fix her own meals without any support or help from you. It just won't happen because preparing a healthful meal or snack is not a priority for her. It is your responsibility to supervise or coordinate the meal preparation.
- Fill the refrigerator with healthful foods.
- Work more fresh foods into your meals: vegetables, fruit, salads, cold sandwiches. It can also reduce the time you spend preparing meals—a blessing when you have young children.
- Let family members decide when they're full. Don't insist that they take more servings or that they must clean their plates.
- Introduce a new dish once each week during the transitional time. Serve it at a time when the family is rested and receptive. Accompanying the new dish should be items that are family favorites. For the rest of the week, serve meals that are more familiar to your family.
- Keep all the recipes for new dishes in one place, where you can easily find them.
- Ask your family for feedback: What did they like? What meals would they change? Then take their ideas into account as you plan next week's menu.
- Get other people involved. Suggest to your friends that they try out some new recipes, too. Then invite them over for a potluck and share ideas.
- When no one eats much, don't criticize or blame them or yourself. But, when your new dishes go over well, offer praise and encouragement.
- Be light about the changes you're trying to make. Keep your sense of humor, and be the first to crack a joke about the meal that just didn't work.

Gearing up for long-term changes in the way you eat. The presence of chronic illness in any member usually changes nutrition for the whole family. What's more, those changes can be far-reaching over the years. Instead of letting this process happen randomly, take charge.

Everyone knows that simply gathering more information is not enough to change behavior. This fact is simple to verify: Look at people who know the risks of smoking and yet are unable to quit the habit. Or consider the person with high blood cholesterol who can recite, in detail, all the facts about heart disease, but who still loads up on fast food cheeseburgers, malts, and fries three nights a week.

To really change behavior, other factors must be at work. First among them is a clear objective—one that can be achieved in the short term. After that objective is reached, a new one can be substituted, building in steps toward the long-term goal. Another factor is awareness of exactly when behavior deviates from the objective. Add to this a third factor: rewards for achieving each objective.

With these three elements in place, you have a workable system for changing any personal habit. How do you translate that into changing eating habits? Consider this: Ask yourself some questions. First: How do I want our family to eat? What foods do we need to add to our meals to help our child control chronic illness? What foods do we need to delete? This step yields your long-term goals for nutrition.

Holidays without junk food. Christmas, Easter, New Year's, the Fourth of July, Hanukkah, or Halloween—these occasions offer the supreme test for your new eating habits. Again, it helps if you don't view this as a burden or threat. There are times when you can relax your standards, and your health care team can help you with this.

Prevent problems. Do a little homework before the holidays: Think of some alternatives to hot dogs, sweet rolls, egg nog, donuts, alcohol, marshmallows, potato chips, and other holiday tempters.

Be creative. For Halloween, encourage your children to trade their candy for another reward, such as a movie. They can also collect for UNICEF or donate foods to food shelves and hospitalized children. Give sugar-free gum to trick-or-treaters. Put small gifts—toys, books— in the Easter basket instead of food.

Working with Your Health Care Team

It's essential for you to establish a good working relationship with your child's health care team. We say "team" because you'll be working with several kinds of medical professionals: Physicians, nurses, dietitians, family therapists, lab technologists, rehabilitation specialists, and others. Together they'll design a plan of care for your child.

Remember, you are the key player on the health care team. The success of any plan depends on how well the family is able to carry it out at home. Parents need to tell the health care team what things they will realistically be able to do. Learning how to speak up to doctors and say "I can't do that because," or "I don't understand what you mean," while it may seem difficult, is really the best approach to helping your child. So be honest about what you can handle and what you don't understand.

Parents also need to be present at the clinic visits and to be active, but not overly active, participants in the plan. Make time for adequate discussion. Think about what your concerns are in advance. Don't leave until they are discussed.

As you work with the health care team, you'll draw on the same basic skill you use in raising your children: striking a balance between qualities that seem like opposites. You want to be assertive, ask questions, express your doubts and concerns, and make sure your child gets the best possible care. At the same time, you need to listen, cooperate, and follow the plan of care that has been developed, using your input.

To help you find this balance, we offer the following suggestions. Part of what follows is based on material developed by PATHFINDER, a division of the International Diabetes Center. PATHFINDER develops community networks for children with chronic illness or physical handicaps.

Communicate with your health care team – and your child. Your description of your child's condition will help the physician and others as they plan treatment in an atmosphere of harmony and respect. You will need to be frank, organized, and clear about the information you bring to your health care team. Do your best to talk with your team about things that can't easily be explained.

It's also critical that you communicate clearly with another person: your child. Every visit to a health care provider will register in your child's mind and heart. Young children, especially, will mirror your reactions: If you feel discomfort, your child may well feel the same. If you establish a good relationship with the health care team, this makes it easier for your child to do so.

Remember, too, when it comes to observing adult reactions, your child may have an ability resembling ESP. Sometimes the most subtle clue – a pursed lip, a wavering voice – is all your child needs to figure out that you're upset.

This is the hardest part for many parents. As one mother said, "On the one hand, I'm told to be open about my feelings and not hide anything. But if I show any sign of anxiety, my child becomes anxious, too. Where's the balance between being honest and being gentle with my child?"

Balancing love and honesty. In answering this question, we're reminded once again of balancing opposites. No, you cannot and should not hide your reactions. On the other hand, telling everything you think and feel is often just too much for a child to handle.

The best answer we have is: When talking to your child, be open about your reactions to diagnosis and treatment. But respond in a way that's appropriate to the child's age and understanding. You can be honest without revealing every detail of your thoughts and emotions or offering medical details that bewilder your child.

If the outcome of a treatment is uncertain, you can say so; if you're afraid, you can often say that, too. But always balance this admission with a positive statement: "Sometimes I worry a lot about this illness. I know you do, too. But, remember that I plan to be with you whenever you need me."

Often what a young child may fear most is not the outcome of a chronic illness—something that's often uncertain and abstract anyway. Rather, the child fears being alone, without a reliable adult caregiver. When things get rough, reaffirm your relationship: Let the child know that someone he trusts will "be there" when it counts. Then keep your promise.

Finally, go beyond the bare facts when talking to your child about diagnosis, treatments, and medical appointments. Offer praise when your child follows the plan of care. Provide rewards, too—a video tape, a movie, a treasured toy. True, you can't schedule joy; however, you can make space for it in your lives.

Turn to one person first. It's important to have one health care professional who knows your child well. This professional, your primary care provider, may be a local pediatrician, family physician, nurse practitioner, or another staff member at your local clinic.

The primary care provider has two functions. One, this is the person you turn to first. Second, this provider helps you coordinate the different services your child needs.

Choose a primary care provider carefully. This is one of the most crucial decisions you'll make. Amazingly enough, some parents drift toward a primary provider by chance, hearsay, or cursory opinion. There's a smarter way to do it.

Before you draw up a list of names, do some thinking. What do you want from a primary care provider? What's most important to you? Someone with a specialized knowledge of your child's condition? Someone who listens well? Someone who excels at giving emotional support? Someone who explains facts calmly and clearly?

Next, apply your powers of observation. You should try to meet with a potential provider before establishing a long-term relationship. Interview him to determine if he is the best person for this very important job. During that first meeting, look at the way this persons relates to your family. Does she make eye contact with you and your child? Does he talk directly to your child whenever possible instead of using you as a buffer? Does she listen? Does he answer your questions? Does the professional know a lot about your child's illness? Or is this person willing to refer to a specialist as needed? A provider who is open and willing to learn with you is often a "gem."

Establish understanding up front. The most common cause of strained relationships between parents and primary care providers is a difference in what they each expect. You can avoid this by clarifying certain points at the beginning.

Being a primary provider calls for a high level of commitment. This person will be your first line of defense, the medical professional who knows the most about your child. More than that, the primary provider is your ally as you negotiate the health care system and coordinate your child's care.

The first rule is to make sure the person you choose agrees to this role— a basic point, perhaps, but one which many parents overlook.

Next, make it clear what kind of relationship you want with this person. Are you looking for a provider who will answer questions beyond those about your child's immediate condition: questions about growth and development, about emotional conflicts? Do you want someone who takes time to listen to your fears and hopes? Can you call to ask questions you didn't get to during the appointment? Will you be free to ask for second opinions?

Be sure you schedule enough time for yourself and the health care team. Provide care for your other children so you won't be distracted at the visit. If telephone follow-up with the primary provider is important, set up the best times for routine calls. Be sure emergency calls can be taken when needed.

Many parents ask if they can schedule times between regular appointments just to ask questions. Some providers are open to this, others are not. Some charge fees for this time, and others will waive costs. Be sure to ask about this.

Ask, too, about emergency care. Where should your child receive this care? How will your child be transported to this site? What do you consider to be an emergency? Does your primary provider agree? Also, find out what coverage your health insurance offers for emergency care. Insurance policies differ widely on this point.

Remember, you can change doctors. Nothing says you have to stay with the first one you choose—or the second or third. If you hear or know of another doctor, you have a right to explore that possibility. One caution, however: Don't overdo it and doctor "hop."

As your child grows, he will most likely need to change to an adult specialist—usually by age 20 or 21. Anticipate this. Ask your physician's help in the selection process. Changing primary care doctors is difficult for all—the child, the parent, and the doctor—especially when you have all worked together for a long time.

Make the most of your appointment time. Prepare for routine visits. Think through the things you want to tell your provider, and decide what questions to ask. Keep a running list of these between appointments, and include your child's questions, too. Be sure your child's medical history is up-to-date so you can answer the provider's questions.

To make the most of an appointment, some parents hold a mental "dress rehearsal." Picture yourself walking into the provider's office; try to visualize the sequence of events. Practice verbalizing your questions; it often helps to actually try this with a friend.

When you step out of that office or examining room, what do you want to know that you don't know now? What are your specific objectives for this visit? Identify your top three concerns; if there's not time for all your questions, make sure you at least get to these.

Though you may feel awkward about it at first, take notes on what your provider says. The very act of writing will aid your memory of the key points. Also, repeat a question if the answer doesn't make sense at first. Some parents fear doing this; for them, repeating a question is something like admitting incompetence. They feel a need to always appear the expert. However, appearances don't count; clear understanding does.

To start, think about these common concerns. Parents of children with chronic illnesses have many common concerns. Some of these are listed below. Even when a question doesn't apply to you, this list may help focus your thinking. In each question, "you" refers to the primary provider or other member of your health care team.

Initial questions to ask:

- Can you diagnose my child's condition now? If not, how long will we have to wait? Are there any consequences of not having an immediate diagnosis?
- What should we be concerned about immediately? What are our long-term concerns?
- Is this condition stable? Can my child's health improve? Is there a chance it could get worse? How much control do we have over the course of this condition?
- How will this condition affect my child's growth and development?
- Does this condition call for any changes in my parenting style? Will it affect how I set limits for my child? How much direct care will I be responsible for? What self-care can my child handle?
- Will my child need to see a specialist? Why? Will you interpret the results for me? How will the results affect our total plan of care?

Asking about medication, tests, and surgery:

- What medications are you prescribing? What are the side effects? Are there any alternatives? How do we administer the medication, and for how long? Can my child still take cough syrup, aspirin, or aspirin substitutes?

- What is the purpose of each test you recommend? What will it reveal that we don't already know? Will the test be stressful for my child? If so, what can I do about it?

- What is the purpose of any surgery you recommend? What are the long-term effects or possible complications? What follow-up care do you recommend? What will happen if we don't do the surgery?

- How long will my child need to stay in the hospital? Who will be treating my child? Can I stay at the hospital? Can you recommend a program that prepares children for a hospital stay?

- What will this test, treatment, or procedure cost? How much will my insurance cover?

Referrals to a Specialist. If you are referred or want to be referred to a specialist, be sure and clarify the following questions with your primary physician:

- Why is my child seeing the specialist, or why am I seeking this referral?
  - Diagnosis?
  - Another opinion?
  - Ongoing care?

- How frequently does my child need to see the specialist?

- How will the information be transmitted to my primary physician?

- Whom should I call for more information and when?

If there is conflicting information given, be sure and discuss this with your primary physician.

Sometimes your specialist may provide all your child's ongoing care. This is particularly true if you live in the same area as the specialist. If you need to travel some distance, then it's really necessary to establish primary care with someone close to your home.

What you need to tell the team

Parents have an obligation to the health care team to tell them what's going on at home. If the stresses are pushing everyone apart at home and everyone is fighting, or worse yet, not talking, don't say "Everything is fine." Be honest! Don't have unrealistic expectations of the team. Also, don't use the health care providers as "parents" for your child. Never use medical care as a threat. For example, don't tell your child if she doesn't do something, she will have to have more shots or the doctor will be angry with her.

Cooperation and openness are the keys. You are sometimes both coach and quarterback on your health team, but you're never alone when it comes to care for your child. Ask for help and information every time you need it.

Chapter Twelve

· ·

WHEN YOU CAN'T BE THERE: CHILD CARE ISSUES

P arents need to be able to use both child care and babysitter services with confidence. Today, it is more common than not that parents work outside the home. As a matter of fact, 70 percent of American women between the ages of 25 and 40 years old work outside the home, according to current estimates. Therefore, other caring people should and can be trained to take care of the child with chronic illness. This is very important for maintaining the "whole parent."

To use child care effectively, parents must answer two questions:

- How much, in general, will we expect child-care providers to do?
- What specific information does the provider need to manage our child's chronic illness?

In this chapter, we'll explore answers to both these questions.

Clarify What You Expect

Whether parents elect to use day-care centers, babysitters, or live-in nannies, they can often expect to pay large percentages of their salaries for child care. They, therefore, have a right to expect certain services for this payment. As a general rule, however, no extra assessments should be charged to you because your child has a chronic illness, unless, of course, the care provider must supply extra food items or supplies.

As a parent, it is basically your responsibility to inform and support your child-care provider no matter which form of care you select. This is true for every parent who uses child care, but when your child has a chronic illness, the issue is more pressing.

All parents have different styles for doing nearly everything. In the case of child care, the ways of working with a care provider will vary from parent to parent, and probably will vary greatly. The styles in which parents explain what they expect of the child-care provider, however, we can illustrate with three very different approaches:

- The "worriers"
- The "dumpers"
- The "collaborators"

The worriers. These parents are very anxious about child care in any form. They worry that the child will not receive enough special attention. Their concerns are expressed in questions such as: "What if my child needs help immediately and no one notices?" "What happens when my child doesn't eat a full lunch or eat on time?"

Too often, however, the worriers miss an important point: Their concerns are basically the same as any parent who leaves a child with a "stranger." For almost every parent, this feeling is the same: "No one can care for my child as well as I can." And this feeling is normal.

The anxiety of the worrier, however, may be coupled with guilt about using child-care services in the first place. We receive a powerful message from many sources (including grandparents): "If your child has a chronic illness, then a parent, the mother, should stay at home until the child starts school." This opinion fails to consider the practical and financial pressures faced by all parents today.

You can spot the worriers when you see certain behaviors. For one, saying goodbye becomes an elaborate ritual. These parents do not just "drop off" the child at the home or child-care center. Instead, they stay for a long time to watch the child, they go over specific details again and again, and they try to make sure the child is completely settled and happy before they leave. Understandably, when this parent arrives at the workplace, he or she is mentally exhausted from this daily separation process.

When an incident involving the child of the "worrier" parent occurs—say when a child with diabetes has blood sugar levels of more than 300 at noon—these parents demand to know what went wrong. The worriers may lose all perspective, forgetting that the situation is not life-threatening, and that it is futile to place blame for every instance of high blood sugar.

Too often, fears of these worriers are contagious. The child-care provider may constantly fear something disastrous is about to happen—and that he or she will be blamed. Soon, the child picks up on all these fears and begins to manipulate, to seek attention, and to "get away with things" because of everyone's anxiety.

The pressures felt by the child-care provider often result in the shortening of these relationships. If the parent expects too much of the provider, the provider is likely to tell the family to make other arrangements.

The dumpers. These parents are the opposite of the worriers. Dumpers do little or nothing to help the child-care provider. In effect, they say: "My child is your charge completely. That's what I'm paying you for. I've done my job and now I'm off to work to do another job."

It's difficult to say what's behind this attitude. Perhaps these parents haven't accepted the fact their child has a chronic illness. This is unfortunate, but must be faced squarely.

The dumpers drop off their child hastily in the morning. They don't take time to give the child-care provider the necessary instructions or supplies and don't replenish them when asked. What's more, they are often late to pick up the child—and rarely do they offer explanations.

When something does go wrong—for example, when a child has a fight with another child—these parents may not seem to care. Or, they may immediately blame the provider or other child. Dumpers are quick to judge what's gone wrong and slow to give any positive reinforcement or information.

The collaborators. These parents represent what most of us should strive to achieve. Collaborators are positive and confident. They believe other people can adequately care for a child with chronic illness when given the right information and support, and they take the time to inform and support the provider.

Still, collaborators are not dreamers; they're in touch with their fears and concerns about child care. They understand and accept that there are alternative ways to care for their child. True, the child care provider will do things differently—such as serve different kinds of meals—but they understand that no one style of care has to be best.

These parents are usually easy to identify. To begin with, they schedule a quiet time with the provider to discuss the child's needs, schedule, and care. This is done at the outset and at least twice each year, and certainly when anything changes. Collaborators respond to the provider's needs, questions, and apprehensions. They make certain to leave office numbers and forwarding numbers. They drop off and pick up their children on time. Finally, they offer and bring suggestions for snacks and birthday treats that can be shared by all the children.

Collaborators teach the child care provider necessary skills and information, such as how to use the blood glucose monitor, how to administer medication, what to do in an emergency. They may make arrangements and offer to pay for a CPR class for the child care provider. They offer printed materials on the child's illness and answer questions whenever they come up. Most importantly, they provide the child's physician's phone number and authorize the provider to call the doctor if parents are not available. Overall, these behaviors tell the provider, "We value your work and commitment to care for our child."

Provide Specific Information

To become a collaborator, you must share the essential information about your child's chronic illness with your child care provider. Do this regularly—at least two times per year. The following is an outline of what to cover:

Medication. Explain how to administer medication. Make sure anyone who cares for your child knows the key facts: the name of the medication, dosage, times it's administered, and how it's administered (by mouth, by injection, and so on).

Meal plan. Many children with chronic illness have a diet similar to that of other children their age. However, treats should be given only with the parent's permission. Also, give your provider guidelines on snacks, meal size, timing, and content.

Exercise. Children need exercise each day. It's a good idea to encourage supervised activity or play after snacks or meals—not right before lunch. Snacks should be planned for and packed if any field trips are scheduled.

What to do in an emergency. Children with chronic illness may experience conditions that need to be treated right away, such as an insulin reaction, asthma episodes, or seizures. If this is true for your child, give detailed instructions for the action needed in these situations. Ideally, you should schedule a separate time to do this—not, for example, just when you're dropping off or picking up your child for the day. Also, schedule a refresher session at least twice a year where you review the action plan.

How to reach you. Give a physician or health care provider's phone number to your child care provider. This information should be posted near a phone and easy to find. Tell the child care provider to call the physician whenever a question arises and you can't be reached. In an emergency, ask the provider to call any physician. Alert the child's physician to this possibility.

Tips for Using Babysitters

Parents need to use babysitters to get away. They should not feel guilty about asking someone else to care for the child with a chronic illness. Working outside the home is not the only legitimate reason to use child care. There can be many others, including those times when you just "need a break."

Some parents of children with diabetes only allow themselves a break once a year when they send their kids off to diabetes camp. This is simply not enough!

Finding Good Babysitters

Locating the best person to care for your child when you need to be away can be difficult. One of the best ways is the old word-of-mouth technique. Ask about other babysitters in your neighborhood. Who would your friends choose? Keep your eyes open for neighborhood teenage girls and boys, single men and women, and retired couples. Find out where they live. Call them and ask for references.

Schools and community centers offer "Babysitter Classes." Call the school or center and talk with the instructor. Get names and recommendations from the instructor.

Churches and Sunday School centers also may be able to help you. Get involved in a nursery program and ask about people who are available and who have any experience in taking care of a child with your child's illness.

Arrange for a babysitting exchange with friends. Once a month offer to take care of each family's children in exchange for a similar service. Also, call on relatives and your "extended family" when you need a break.

What to Tell the Sitter

When you do leave your child, be sure you specify when you want to be called. Give the sitter examples of situations in which you would want to be called. Review the appropriate use of the "911" emergency telephone service. Tell the sitter when it is appropriate to call 911. Be sure to inform babysitters exactly how to use medications. Go over the medication routine step by step, ask the sitter to explain the medication routine back to you, and then review until you're comfortable that the sitter understands. Before you have someone babysit for your child, invite her over for an evening during the usual hours she might be sitting for you. Go over the normal concerns you would have with a sitter. Give her a tour of your house, explaining how to use kitchen appliances, special equipment for the child's illness, use of the telephone (including how you want him to answer the phone), where light switches are, use of door locks, etc. Ask how much she usually charges and be prepared to pay accordingly.

Following bedtime routines is always important, especially when these include medications, use of humidifiers, special toileting, or the like. Show the babysitter all the steps. Help him anticipate behavior and discipline issues. Explain in front of the child what behaviors should be expected and what discipline should be. Convey confidence that she can handle things appropriately.

When you find someone you and your child like, arrange in advance (for example, when he's leaving your first meeting) when you would like him to come again. Many parents choose one night a month and "book" the babysitter automatically. When handled this way, everyone can count on it and parents can look forward to another evening out.

Good Preparation

Child-care experiences from the preschool years will stay with you and your child as he enters school. As you find ways that work—ways to communicate, ways to support, ways to solve problems, and ways to feel involved in your child's day—bring these with you into the school-aged years with a sense of confidence that you and your child will succeed in adjusting easily to the school experience.

Chapter Thirteen

. . . .

WORKING WITH THE SCHOOL STAFF

E very child needs to be fully involved in school activities. And this is especially so for the child with a chronic illness. Participation reduces the child's sense of being "different" and hopefully minimizes those feelings of isolation. Moreover, there is likely to be a direct relationship between the number of days your child misses school due to the health condition and how well the child adjusts to school in general.

In a sense, many chronic illnesses are "invisible." Often there are no outward signs: no wheelchair, no crutches, no other visible signal that the child has special health needs. When this is the case, there must be a plan for the right kind of medical attention to be given in the school setting.

What happens when a student with a chronic illness doesn't get attention? When hypoglycemia, a seizure, or an asthma episode consistently forces a child to leave class, avoid sports, or cancel after-school activities? What if no one at school knows what to do when one of these occurs? For one, the child is at risk for serious physical consequences. Beyond that, he could lose social contact with other students; she may lose ground academically, as well. As a result, this child may need special services: tutoring, special education testing, or some other kind of assessment.

The best solution for this child is for the parents to work closely with the staff at the child's school, making sure that school experiences are consistent with the care plan. This chapter offers some suggestions on just how to do that, focusing on educational planning, meetings with an educational team, special services, assessments, and similar issues. Not all of this may be relevant to you and your child, but, even if you don't need the full range of services your school offers, you should know what they are.

First, Come to Terms with Your Own Feelings

When we talk about helping your child get the most out of school, we naturally focus on the child and the school staff—mainly the classroom teacher and the school nurse. However, there's another person we need to consider: You.

Having a child with a chronic illness in school raises many issues, along with which may come some very strong feelings: "Who will know what to do if my child has a medical emergency?" "Nobody can care for my child like I do." "Who do I go to when I have a question about my child's activities at school?" "Can I trust anyone there?" "I'll just be worrying about my child all the time." "Why do things seem to go better during the school day and worse when my child is at home?" "Maybe the school can get my child to test and follow his meal plan better than I can."

The first step in adjusting is to take care of yourself: Get these feelings out in the open. There are several advantages to doing so:

1. You can reduce any fear or anxiety about your child being in school.
2. You can examine any of your feelings of inadequacy or anger that someone else might also be able to care for your child.
3. You can defuse small issues now—before they grow into major problems.
4. You can help your child. Your child takes cues from you. When she senses that you are more relaxed and accepting of the school environment, she can relax too.

For these reasons, getting a handle on your fears and doubts will bring good results in the long run. This does not mean it will be easy. In fact, getting in touch with your fears and worries may cause them to feel stronger at first. So don't go it alone. Get some help.

There are several ways to get help: talking openly with your spouse or partner, talking to your physician or other health care provider, or seeing a counselor. If you have a health insurance plan, find out if it covers such services or offers referrals. If you belong to a health maintenance organization (HMO), find out if it offers classes on coping with chronic illnesses. Also, check into support or self-help groups where you can talk to other parents of children with chronic illnesses. Your child's health care team can help you with this.

Advocating for Your Child: Make Your Feelings Known

Be an advocate for your child at school. In many cases, both federal and state laws mandate a clear right for children with chronic illness: the right to an education in the least restrictive, most appropriate setting. Among other things, this means cooperating with your child's efforts to manage a chronic illness.

What, specifically, do we mean? In short, you have the right to ask for the following things:

- **Ask that the school follow the care plan for your child.**

  You can help a lot by making it clear exactly what this requires. Plan realistically for diet, meal schedules, blood or urine testing, exercise, limits on after-school activity, and the like. Don't let this information just sit in a file somewhere. In addition to writing these requirements down, go over them verbally with the child present. Also, ask your child if he's being cared for according to plan.

- **Ask the school staff to cooperate with you.**

  Certain signs show that this cooperation is taking place: the educational team meets promptly and follows your child's educational plan; all of your child's teachers are informed about your child's needs; medications are given on time and in the right dosages; the school nurse contacts you promptly if any emergency occurs.

  When these things are not taking place, then you're not getting the cooperation you need. Don't let this slide. Ask for a primary contact at school—a person to call first when you have a question about your child. Then stay in touch.

- **Ask the school staff members to recognize you and your child as the experts regarding your child's condition.**

  Your child lives with her condition 24 hours each day; you come a close second. Both of you are experts in coping with a chronic illness, and that gives you a perspective even the most well-trained teacher or administrator doesn't have.

  It's important to clarify what the word "expert" means here. It means being highly skilled in a particular area. It does not mean saying that you know everything. Be willing to admit that you don't know it all, but ask the staff to recognize your current ways of living with the illness. These people should take into account your limitations and your strengths.

  School nurses and school personnel cannot legally act on a parent's verbal recommendations or requests for medical care at school. Written orders from the child's physician must be completed describing the medication and how it is to be given or treatment to be done at school, with signatures provided by the doctor and the parents. Plan for this each school year.

- **Ask the school to support self-care.**

  First, define how much responsibility your child can handle in managing his own condition: Can he be trusted to take medication on time? If she has diabetes, can she monitor her own blood glucose levels, given the right equipment? Can he sense when he's had too much exercise in gym and when he needs to treat an insulin reaction?

  Once you've answered these questions and talked them over with your child, write up a list of her responsibilities. Go over this list with your primary contact at school, get written orders for medications and treatments from your doctor as needed, and ask the educational team to act according to the list. Be sure to ask for feedback on how well your child is doing so you can change your child's level of responsibility and participation in self-care if necessary.

  In time, you may need to change your thinking a little. Perhaps your child can take more responsibility; perhaps she needs to wait a year before handling certain tasks. That's okay. Just adjust your plan. The important thing is that the school supports your overall effort to foster self-care.

Keep Track of Your Questions

It helps greatly if you get organized and keep careful records about your child's care plan. Keep track of your questions, not only about your child's health care but about his school experience, as well. One of the best ways to do this is using a journal, a notebook, or a tape-recorder—one that's easy to carry with you. The main requirement is that your journal be something you can reach for in your car, at your office, in the kitchen—any place you'll be when a question or observation occurs to you.

Whatever system you use should be flexible, allowing you to jot down questions and ideas at the moment they come to you. It should also allow you to make further notes, such as the answers your child's classroom teacher gave you to questions. Keep a running list of questions. Your best ideas may come when you're fixing dinner, watching TV, mowing the yard, or driving to work—times when you're not specifically thinking about your child. Value these moments of insight. Don't forget to list your child's questions. Work on phrasing the questions in terms meaningful to him. Later, carefully explain the answer you received or any further action that needs to be taken.

Considerations for the School Staff

Consider for a moment how school personnel—such as teachers, principals, and office staff—may react to caring for a child with a chronic illness. The majority of these people want to do everything they can to help your child have a rich school experience. Yet, they may struggle with certain doubts about caring for the child with chronic illness—just as you did.

In many cases, the teacher may already have had experience caring for a child with a specific chronic illness. This experience, positive or negative, will affect how she will interact with your child. Or, perhaps the whole concept of your child's chronic illness is new or threatening to the teachers. They already may feel some pressure from their expanding roles and responsibilities. Curriculums are expanding to include drug education, AIDS education, and self-esteem training. Adding concerns about medications or medical emergencies may seem like too much for them at times—especially with the declining numbers of full-time school nurses.

Remind yourself that the school teachers are the education experts. They are very tuned in to the educational, social, and individual needs of children and they respond to all these needs in and out of the classroom on a daily basis. When they report that your medical expectations are seriously interfering with your child's learning, stop and reexamine what you are expecting, what your child is expecting, and how this is affecting his behavior and participation in the classroom.

Keep in mind that attitudes toward children with chronic illness are changing—both in schools and in society at large. Schools are working with more and more children with chronic illness because of the increasing prevalence of these children in the public schools. You may see certain evidence of this in some schools: classrooms with desks arranged to permit room for wheelchairs; public health professionals hired as consultants to the schools; more training, workshops, and in-services on chronic illness; school cafeterias that make allowances for special diets. In short, today's students and teachers may already be adjusted to the sight of a classmate in a wheelchair or the presence of a child who takes medication between classes.

However, you may not always find instant support in your schools. Not every school has an enlightened principal: Some are bogged down in paperwork, rules, and the red tape typical of any bureaucracy. Still you can expect your child to be treated conscientiously.

Perhaps you can't change attitudes overnight. But you can have an impact. How? By giving the key people at school the tools they need: information, guidelines, medical supplies, speedy answers to questions, and respect for their work.

Get Down to Specific Issues

In general, to help your child get the most out of school, you need to:
- Provide teachers and administrators with realistic and specific guidelines on caring for your child in the school setting.
- Provide general information on your child's condition.
- "Be there" when your child needs you and when the school needs you. This means actively working with the school nurse, teacher, health aide, principal, and anyone else who has regular contact with your child at school.
- Provide information on the following topics:

- What food your child needs to eat–and when.
- Any medical supplies required–such as blood testing for children with diabetes.
- Taking part in sports and extracurricular activities.
- Specific conditions that require an immediate response from people at school. Examples are medical emergencies such as a seizure or asthma episode.
- Where and how to reach you during the school day. What to do if you can't be reached.
- How to handle brief illnesses. For example, a child who vomits once or has a single episode of diarrhea may not have to be sent home. Instead, the school nurse or health aide may treat the child with rest, quiet or fluids. After a brief time, the child may be able to return to class.
- How to monitor a specific condition. For example, many schools have blood glucose meters for children with diabetes. These meters can indicate when blood sugar is low–vital information when the child is feeling mildly ill, or during acute episodes. It's the child's choice whether to test regularly.

Share Information with the Whole Educational Team

Foster a team approach to managing your child's chronic illness at school. After all, several people may be working with your child: a school nurse, social worker, classroom teacher, coach, or principal. In addition, your child may see tutors, specialists (such as physical education and music teachers), special education teachers, bus drivers, and more.

All these people make up what we call the educational team. Common sense is the rule here: Since several people will be involved in your child's education, make sure they know about your child's care plan.

When you share information with one person at school, the other people on the team need to get it, too. For example, it doesn't make sense when the nurse, who is at school just two days each week, is the only person who knows how to treat an asthma episode; the physical education teacher needs this skill also. Likewise, the classroom teacher needs to know that lack of attention or blurred vision may be signs of an insulin reaction.

Logically, the best way to foster a team approach is to "pool" your child's health information into some kind of central source. Most importantly, the information should be available in writing—not in someone's head—and it should be based on careful, daily observation of your child, if that's needed. Finally, everyone who works with your child at school should know about this source and use it.

Several kinds of documents currently exist for this purpose. They have names such as an Individualized Health Plan, Pupil Health Record, or Individualized Education Plan. Find out what your child's school uses. Don't assume that the document—if it exists—is still in use or accurate. Ask to see it, plan to discuss it with the educational team, and insist that it be used. What will this document include? This may vary widely among school districts. Common elements are:

- Statements about how the child is currently performing in school.
- A list of goals for the student, along with specific objectives to achieve those goals. These may be called "behavioral objectives" or "instructional objectives." These may be part of an "education plan" or "management plan."
- A list of services the child will receive, including the dates those services will start and end.
- A plan to find out if objectives are being met. The most common term for these is "evaluation criteria."

Frequently, the standard procedure for using this document calls for regular meetings to monitor your child's educational plan. This is where you'll work most directly with members of the educational team. It's also your right to call additional meetings of this team if you have a concern that calls for a coordinated response.

Classroom teachers may be the most important contributors to the planning document. Why? Because they see your child more than anyone else at school. These teachers are often the first to notice changes in health, behavior, or performance. You need to know about these changes—especially if they relate to your child's chronic condition. Other members of the educational team need to know about them, too.

Of course, there are other key sources of health information. These include:

- Interviews with your family.
- Observations by the school nurse.

- Results of tests given at school. These include hearing tests, vision tests, and basic skills tests.
- Information from the child's physician and other health care providers.

All this information should be up to date, kept in a central place and accessible to you. Just as importantly, everyone on the educational team needs to stay current with the information.

Remember one vitally important point: You know your child best. Many people work with your child at school, but ultimately you and your child are in charge of the school experience.

Go to One Person First

After pointing out how important the team is, we're going to stress what may seem like a contradictory point. It's best if you have one person to go to first. Chances are this person will be the classroom or homeroom teacher—though it may be the school nurse, principal, or someone else.

Ideally, this person should be someone you can trust, someone who knows the administrative ropes, and a person who will "work the system" for you. This person's main job is following through—making sure your question is answered, that your issue makes the meeting agenda, and that decisions are backed up with action.

Handling Referrals and Special Services

Someone may feel your child's chronic illness requires some kind of special service from the school. Some of these are:
- Tutoring or some other form of individual or small-group attention
- Special education
- Programs for gifted and talented children
- Intelligence testing
- Counseling

The person who asks for such a service can be you, a teacher, a school nurse, an administrator, or another person from the school district.

Moreover, referral for a special service can happen whether or not chronic illness is a factor.

If someone does request a special service or referral for your child, you can expect a certain series of events to occur. The main players in these events are you, your child, the educational team, and your child's health care team. Everyone's experience is different, but here is a typical sequence:

1. A referral. This is a formal, written acknowledgment that your child has a special need. You can make the referral; so can a teacher or other school staff member. If someone other than you makes the referral, you should be notified first.

2. An evaluation. This merely means that people at school—what we've called the education team—try to find out as much as possible about your child's situation. In some cases, it may mean medical tests, psychological tests, or interviews with your child and family. Just as with the referral, someone from the school district should tell you when an evaluation is being made.

This seems like a lot of activity, and it may take up a lot of your time—not to mention your child's time. The child's physician may be called upon to provide information, too. Keep in mind, though, that the purpose of all this is to answer one basic question: Does your child really need some kind of special service from the school?

3. A meeting to follow up on the evaluation. Here, the members of the team decide whether your child needs special services. The decision—and any recommendations that come with it—must usually be written up in a report and sent to an administrator in the school district. That person might be a superintendent or director of special education, for example.

Before the meeting, contact a local organization that works with your child's chronic illness. These organizations are called advocacy groups, and they exist for many chronic illnesses, including asthma, diabetes, and epilepsy. Ask your health care team to put you in contact with one, or ask if they can provide that service directly. See if someone from the group can attend the evaluation meeting as a representative for your child.

In any case, make sure you get a copy of the final report from this meeting. If you have questions, go to your primary contact on the educational team. If you don't agree with the team's decision, you should ask for someone else to evaluate your child.

4. A meeting to plan for any special services. This happens if you, your child, and the team agree that such a service is needed. Again, the plan will eventually be written up formally as an Individual Education Plan (IEP) or some document with a similar name.

Be sure to go to this planning meeting. If you can't attend, ask to participate by phone. Just make sure you find out what the team is planning for your child. Ask questions. If you have any concerns or doubts about the services planned for your child, make them known.

Once the team settles on a special service for your child, they'll present it to you. Again, be sure that everything is clear to you. Ask specific questions:

- What services will your child receive, and how long will they last?
- What are the goals for your child? Also, find out how those goals will be accomplished through the special service, and how the team will know if goals have actually been reached.
- How will transportation be handled, if any service requires your child to leave school?
- How long will the special service last? If a new plan for service will be drawn up for the future, find out exactly when that's supposed to happen.

More about Testing

Chances are you had vision and hearing tests when you were in school. Today these are still used, along with a range of other tests for many different purposes. As with referrals and special services, such tests may be a part of your child's school experience–or they may not. Chronic illness is not the sole deciding factor influencing their use.

What follows is a partial list of these tests. Keep in mind, too, that some tests may overlap: A single test might cover several of the areas mentioned below. Or several tests might focus on the same skill.

- *Achievement tests.* These measure what your child has already learned. Examples are basic skills tests or benchmark tests in subjects such as reading, writing, and math.

- *Intelligence tests.* These are different than achievement tests, which try to measure what your child has already learned. Intelligence tests, on the other hand, look at what your child can learn in the future. They measure things such as problem solving, memory, and the ability to classify things and ideas. Examples are the Stanford-Binet Intelligence (IQ) Test and the Wechsler Intelligence Scale for Children (WISC).
- *Screening tests.* Basically, these are a kind of "pre-test": They help determine if more testing is needed in a certain area. The Minnesota Child Development Inventory is this type of test; so is the Denver Developmental Screening Test
- *Language tests.* These try to get at what your child knows by looking at language—what the child can communicate. If your child takes one of these tests, he may be asked to perform a language task—for example, to make up a story to go along with a picture. The tester will listen for how well your child pronounces words, what words she chooses, and what concepts she can explain.

Not all these tests require that the child talk, however. Children who cannot talk may take a test that only requires them to point to pictures, matching those pictures with words or sentences.

How to Work with Your Child's Teacher

Remembering just a few guidelines can improve the relationship between you and your child's teacher, especially when your child has a chronic illness. Some of the most important of these are:
- Make one thing clear: You do not expect the teacher to be a medical professional. The teacher does not have to manage the overall treatment plan for your child or understand the details of the chronic illness.
- Reaffirm the teacher's role. Tell her you understand that she is an education professional, which means she is trained to be sensitive to the unique educational needs of children. Let her know you know your child is one of many who require her attention.
- Express your appreciation when you see the teacher is cooperating with you. If, on the other hand, a teacher is not following the instructions for managing your child's condition, then ask how you can help. Offer to answer questions, and set up a specific time to do so.

- Schedule a conference with the teacher shortly after classes begin—or shortly after your child's illness is diagnosed. Clarify what you expect and what help you'll provide. Go over the Individual Health Plan or other basic planning document your school uses.

- Make sure the teacher knows what to do in a health-related emergency.

How to Manage Medication at School

In many ways, it's best to arrange things so your child goes through the school day without having to take medication. Emphasize this point with your physician and pharmacist.

Still, many children have no choice: they must take medication at school. If your child is one who must, take certain steps to make sure everything goes smoothly.

Make sure the right people know. The first person to tell is your child, of course. Beyond this, however, you should identify who on the school staff needs to know about medication. Depending on the school, this may be the principal, school nurse, classroom teacher, gym teacher—or perhaps all these people.

Get a complete prescription. Get one copy for yourself and another one for school. This prescription should clearly state that your child has to take medication during the school day.

Give your permission. Your school may already have a standard form for this purpose. This form should list who will give medication to your child, and it should state that this person has your permission to do so.

Get a duplicate bottle. Expecting your child to cart medication to and from school can be asking too much. The easiest thing is to get two bottles of medication—one for school and one for home. Ask your pharmacist about this.

Make sure bottles are properly labeled. Prescription bottles should be labeled with the:
- Pharmacy name
- Child's name

- Physician's name
- Name of the medication
- Dosage to be given
- How it is to be given (by mouth, injection, etc.)

Beyond this, it's a good idea to list possible side effects from the medication.

Ask for follow-up. Ask that whoever gives medication to your child keeps records. Again, your school may already have a procedure for this. If not, ask that records be kept for your child. To find out how well the medication is working, your physician needs an accurate record of when medication was given and in what doses.

These records should also note other important facts: Did the teacher note any change in your child's behavior with the medication? Does the medication affect your child's attention span? Are symptoms under control? Is your child taking any medication without your permission? These are the kind of questions the record should answer.

Make sure medication is stored correctly. For maximum safety, medication should be stored at the proper temperature, in the proper container, and in an appropriate place – one that can be locked. Only people with your permission should have access to your child's medication.

Last, but not Least: The Bus Driver

Bus drivers are often the first and last school staff member to see your child each day. They can witness and be responsible for your child during significant times of the day. Parents need to be sure their child's relevant medical information is communicated to these important people and that problems and needs be communicated back to the parent. Parents should ask at the beginning of each school year the best way to do this. Should it be done by the school nurse, the parent directly, or some other designated person?

Behavior problems and unhealthy peer relationships such as teasing or bullying often show up on the school bus. If you suspect this, arrange for some assistance and discipline from the bus driver. Usually these drivers are responsible to the principal of the school, so you may need to communicate through that channel.

Finally

Remember: Your child spends a major part of his day in the school setting. Many of these experiences can have a major impact on your child and how he is going to accept his chronic illness and, ultimately, himself. Think carefully and seriously about how you can help make the school experience a positive one. Avoid setting up sides—us versus the school. You, your child, and the school are all on the same team . . . hopefully working together toward the same goal: making your child's educational experience the best and most beneficial for her future independence.

Epilogue

A great deal of information has been presented in this book. We hope that it will enable you to realize that raising a child with chronic illness does not require unusual parenting, but that the unique challenges of chronic disease do make positive parenting more difficult.

We've asked you to look at yourself honestly. It takes courage to reflect on and examine how you were parented. Of that information, you need keep only what fits your marriage and family life. It takes both courage and self-discipline to eliminate from your repertoire what doesn't fit. And, it takes compassion to forgive what—you now probably recognize—was the less than perfect parenting skill of your own parents.

We've reminded you that it takes careful time management and organization to balance the many roles you are asked to play. But, we've also urged you to prioritize so that important adult relationships—between you and your spouse or partner—can be nurtured as fully as you nurture your children. We've tried to emphasize the importance of taking care of yourself and of dealing openly with your fears and anxiety about parenting your child.

We've talked about communication and its importance in keeping the other relationships in your child's life open: with grandparents, babysitters, day-care providers, teachers, school nurses, the entire health care team, and even the school bus driver. And we've talked a lot about consistency.

Our own experiences in working with families of children with chronic illness has taught us that consistent parenting pays off. And we've seen firsthand that consistent parenting requires a confident parent. We hope *Whole Parent, Whole Child* has provided the tools you need for building confidence by enabling you to:
- forgive yourself for any limitations previously perceived;
- admit that you are human and, therefore, imperfect;
- applaud yourself for the sure and certain knowledge that you have always given and will always give it your best shot—and that will always be good enough;

- seek the support you need from people and organizations who are anxious to help you.

We hope you'll remember, too, that your child's job is to move toward independence. Children move at varying speeds and require different levels of support and assistance along the way. We urge you to keep listening to your child and to yourself, and to keep talking along the way as you gradually loosen the ties that bind you together. Those ties will never be totally severed. Yet, you must allow enough slack so they don't chafe your child. They need to be loose enough to allow for healthy risk-taking that will ensure your child's movement is forward and pro-gressive.

Finally, we hope that you've learned a very important principle: That laughter can lighten the load for parents and child alike. More than any-thing, we urge you to share joy with your entire family. Laugh as often as you can.

Congratulations! You have worked your way to the end of this book. We know you and your child will likely gain strength and grow, together. You can be a whole parent. And because of your efforts, reaching out and reaching in, with each other, your child will also be whole.

Resources

· ·

We include here a list of resources for you to draw upon as you learn more about chronic illness in children. This can only be a partial list. However, if you begin with the publications and organizations listed here, they can lead you to more resources.

Keep one point in mind: It's good to read widely. Don't restrict yourself to studying only the literature about your child's particular chronic condition. Even if your child has asthma, for example, you may still find a book about adjusting to diabetes useful. So many of the emotional and family issues are the same, regardless of the particular condition.

Listed below are books on other topics—stress control, relaxation, nutrition, and more. These, too, will be relevant to all chronic conditions.

Books from the Diabetes Center, Inc..

The Joy of Snacks

The Physician Within

Pass the Pepper Please

Fast Food Facts

Convenience Food Facts

Opening the Door to Good Nutrition

Learning to Live WELL with Diabetes

Exchanges for All Occasions

A Guide to Healthy Eating

Managing the School Age Child with a Chronic Health Condition: A Practical Guide

The Diabetes Youth Curriculum: A Toolbox for Educators

You can also order these books by writing to:
Diabetes Center, Inc.
Ridgedale Office Center
Suite 250
13911 Ridgedale Drive
Minneapolis, MN 55343

Other Books

American Diabetes Association. Family Cookbook II. Englewood Cliffs, NJ: Prentice-Hall, 1980.

Benson, Herbert and Klipper, Miriam Z. The Relaxation Response. New York: Avon Books, 1976.

Berends, Polly. Whole Child/Whole Parent: A Spiritual and Practical Guide to Parenthood. New York: Harper & Row, 1983.

Blum, Robert (Ed.). Chronic Illness and Disabilities in Childhood and Adolescence. Orlando, FL: Grune & Stratton, 1984.

Briggs, Dorothy C. Your Child's Self-Esteem: The Key to His Life. New York: Doubleday, 1970.

Brody, Jane. Jane Brody's Nutrition Book. New York: Bantam Books, 1987.

Clarke, Jean. Self-Esteem: A Family Affair. New York: Harper & Row, 1980.

Crary, Elizabeth. Without Spanking or Spoiling: A Practical Approach to Toddler and Preschool Guidance. Seattle, WA: Parenting Press, 1979.

Cuddingan, Maureen and Hanson, Mary Beth. Growing Pains–Helping Children Deal with Everday Problems Through Reading. Chicago: American Library Association, 1988.

Dreikurs, Rudolf and Soltz, Vicki. Children: The Challenge. New York: Dutton, 1964.

Edelwich, Jerry and Brodsky, Archie. Diabetes: Caring for your Emotions as Well as Your Health. Reading, MA: Addison-Wesley, 1986.

Fassler, Joan. Helping Children Cope: Mastering Stress Through Books and Stories. New York: The Free Press, 1978.

Featherstone, Helen. A Difference in the Family: Living with a Disabled Child. New York: Penguin, 1980.

Ginott, Haim. Between Parent and Child. New York: Avon Books, 1969.

Good, Julia Darnell and Reis, Joyce Good. A Special Kind of Parenting. La Leche League, P.O. Box 1209, Franklin Park, IL 60131-8209.

Gordon, Thomas. Parent Effectiveness Training: The Tested New Way to Raise Responsible Children. New York: McKay, 1970.

Hobbs, Nicholas. The Futures of Children: Recommendations of the Project on Classification of Exceptional Children. San Francisco: Jossey-Bass, 1975.

Hobbs, Nicholas and Perrin, James, (eds.). Issues in the Care of Children with Chronic Illness: A Sourcebook on Problems, Services and Policies. San Francisco: Jossey-Bass, 1985.

Hobbs, Nicholas, Perrin, James and Ireys, Henry (Eds.). Chronically Ill Children and Their Families. San Francisco: Jossey-Bass, 1985.

Kuczen, Barbara. Childhood Stress: How to Raise a Healthier, Happier Child. New York: Delta, 1987.

Kushner, Harold S. When Bad Things Happen to Good People. New York: Avon Books, 1983.

Massie, Robert and Massie, Suzanne. Journey. New York: Ballantine Books.

McDaniel, Sandy and Bielen, Peggy. Project Self-Esteem. Rolling Hills Estates, CA: B.L. Winch and Associates, 1986.

PATHFINDER. How to Develop a Community Network. Minneapolis, MN: 1987.

PATHFINDER. How to Help your Child: A Parent Resource Manual. Eau Claire, WI: 1987.

Pearlman, Laura and Scott, Kathleen. Raising the Handicapped Child. Englewood Cliffs, NJ: Prentice-Hall, 1981.

Pitzele, Sefra K. We Are Not Alone: Learning to Live with Chronic Illness. New York: Workman, 1986.

Plaut, Thomas F. Children with Asthma: A Manual for Parents. Amherst, MA: Pedipress, 1984.

Powell, Thomas H. and Ogle, Peggy Ahrenhold. Brothers and Sisters: A Special Part of Exceptional Families. Baltimore: Paul H. Brookes Publishing Co., 1985.

Reisner, Helen (Ed.). Children with Epilepsy: A Parent's Guide. Kensington, MD: Woodbine House, 1987.

Satir, Virginia. Peoplemaking. Palo Alto, CA: Science and Behavior Books, 1972.

Satter, Ellyn. How to Get Your Kid to Eat . . . But Not Too Much. Palo Alto, CA: Bull Publishing Co., 1987.

Scheiber, Barbara and Moore, Cory. Practical Advice for Parents: A Guide to Finding Help for Children with Handicaps. Montgomery County Association for Retarded Citizens, 11600 Nebel St., Rockville, MD 20852, 1981.

Smith, Sally L. No Easy Answers: The Learning Disabled Child at Home and at School. New York: Bantam, 1981.

Summers, Jean Ann. The Right to Grow Up—An Introduction to Adults with Developmental Disabilities. Baltimore, MD: Paul H. Brookes Publishing Co., 1985.

Magazines and Newsletters

Exceptional Children. The Council for Exceptional Children, 1920 Association Drive, Reston, VA 22091

Parenting. Parenting Magazine Partners, 501 Second Street, San Francisco, CA 94107

Organizations

Organizations are a good source of help. Many of them also offer materials: books, pamphlets, videotapes, slide series, and more. In addition, an organization can often put you in touch with other parents and self-help groups in your area.

Adolescent Autonomy Project
Children's Rehabilitation Center
2270 Ivy Road
Charlotsville, VA 22901

The American Association of Marriage and Family Counselors
225 Yale Avenue
Claremont, CA 91711

American Diabetes Association, Inc.
2 Park Avenue
New York, NY 10016

American Heart Association
7320 Greenville Avenue
Dallas, TX 75231

American Lung Association
1740 Broadway
New York, NY 10019

American Medical Association
535 North Dearborn Street
Chicago, IL 60610

American Psychiatric Association
1200 17th Street, NW
Washington, DC 20036

American Society of Handicapped Physicians
137 Main Street
Grambling, LA 71245

Arizona Consortium for Children with Chronic Illness
P.O. Box 2128
Phoeniz, AZ 85001

Arthritis Foundation
1314 Spring Street NW
Atlanta, GA 30309

Association for the Care of Children's Health
3615 Wisconsin Ave. NW
Washington, DC 20016

Camps for Children with Special Needs and Their Families
Parents' Guide to Accredited Camps
American Camping Association
100 Bradford Woods
Martinsville, IN 46151

Camp Kaleidoscope (for children with chronic illnesses)
P.O. Box 2916
Duke University Medical Center
Durham, NC 27710

Camp Needlepoint
Contact the American Diabetes Association
3005 Ottawa Avenue South
St. Louis Park, MN 55416

Camp Ozawizeniba (for children and youth with epilepsy)
2701 University Avenue, SE
Suite 106
Minneapolis, MN 55406

Camp Superkids
1829 Portland Avenue
Minneapolis, MN 55404

Child and Family Support Project
Children's Hospital Medical Center
4800 Sand Point Way
Seattle, WA 98105

Chronic Illness Teaching Program
Department of Pediatrics and Human Development
B-240, Life Sciences Building
Michigan State University
East Lansing, MI 48824

Clearinghouse on the Handicapped
Office of Special Education and Rehabilitative Services
Department of Education Room
3106 Switzer Building
230 C Street, SW
Washington, DC 20202

Coordination of Care for Chronically Ill Children Program
New York State Department of Health
Tower Building, Room 878
Empire State Plaza
Albany, NY 12237

Division of Maternal and Child Health
U.S. Public Health Service
5600 Fishers Lane
Rockville, MD 20857

Helping Grandparent Program
King County ARC
2230 Eighth Avenue
Seattle, WA 98121

Home-Based Support Services for Chronically Ill Children and Their Families
Tower Building
Room 878
Empire State Plaza
Albany, NY 12237

International Diabetes Center
Park Nicollet Medical Foundation
5000 West 39th Street
Minneapolis, MN 55416

Juvenile Diabetes Foundation
23 East 26th Street
New York, NY 10010

Minnesota Early Learning Design
123 North Third Street
Suite 804
Minneapolis, MN 55401

Muscular Dystrophy Association
810 Seventh Avenue
New York, NY 10019

National Association of Social Workers
1425 H Street, NW, Suite 600
Washington, DC 20005

National Heart and Lung Institute
Bethesda, MD 20014

National Institute of Mental Health
5600 Fishers Lane
Rockville, MD 20852

National Multiple Sclerosis Society
208 East 42nd Street
New York, NY 10017

Parent Advocacy Coalition for Educational Rights (PACER)
4826 Chicago Avenue, South
Minneapolis, MN 55417

Parents Helping Parents, Inc.
535 Race Street
Suite 220
San Jose, CA 95126

Parent Training and Information and Technical Assistance Centers
Central Office
312 Stuart Street, Second Floor
Boston, MA 02116

PATHFINDER
(Improving systems of care for medically vulnerable children)
5000 West 39th Street
Minneapolis, MN 55416

Pilot Parents
2005 North Central
Suite 100
Phoenix, AZ 85004

Sex Information and Education Counsel of the U.S. (SIECUS)
80 Fifth Avenue, Suite 801-2
New York, NY 10011

Sister Kenny Institute
800 East 28th Street
Minneapolis, MN 55407

SKIP—Sick Kids (Need) Involved People
216 Newport Drive
Severna Park, MD 21146

Vocational Guidance and Rehabilitation Services
2289 East 55th Street
Cleveland, OH 44103

Bibliography

Association for the Care of Children's Health. Organizing and Maintaining Support Groups for Parents of Children with Chronic Illness and Handicapping Conditions. Washington, DC: ACCH (3615 Wisconsin Avenue NW, Washington, DC 20016), 1986.

Association for the Care of Children's Health. Parent Resource Directory.

Berne, Eric. Games People Play. New York: Grove Press, 1964.

Bibace, R. and Walsh, M., Eds. Children's Conceptions of Health, Illness, and Bodily Functions. San Francisco, CA: Jossey-Bass, Inc., 1981.

Boehm, A.E. and White, M.A. The Parents' Handbook on School Testing. New York: Teachers College Press, 1982.

Campbell, Ross. How to Really Love Your Teenager. Wheaton, Illinois: Victor Books, 1986.

Campbell, Ross. How to Really Love Your Child. Wheaton, Illinois: Victor Books, 1984.

Canter, Lee. Assertive Discipline for Parents. Santa Monica, CA: Canter and Associates, 1985.

Clemes, Harris and Bean, Reynold. How to Raise Teenagers' Self-Esteem. Los Angeles, CA: Enrich/Price-Stern-Sloan, Inc., 1985.

Cousins, Norman. Anatomy of an Illness: As Perceived by the Patient. New York: W.W. Norton, 1979.

Dobson, James. The Strong Willed Child: Birth Through Adolescence. Wheaton, IL: Tyndale House, 1978.

Dreikurs, Rudolf. Children: The Challenge. New York: Hawthorn/Dutton, 1964.

Eisenberg, M.G., Sutking, L.F. and M.A. Jansen. Chronic Illness and

Disability Through the Life Span: Effects on Self and Family. Vol. 4. New York: Springer Publishing, 1984.

Exceptional Parent, The. Boston: Psy-Ed Corporation & University of Boston School of Education.

Faber, Adele and Mazlish, Elaine. How to Talk So Kids Will Listen and Listen So Kids Will Talk. New York: Avon Books, 1980.

Gortmaker, S.L. and Sappenfield, W. Chronic Childhood Disorders: Prevalence and Impact, Pediatric Clinics of North America, Volume 31 (1984): 3–18.

Harris, Thomas. I'm OK–You're OK: A Practical Guide to Transactional Analysis. New York: Harper & Row, 1967.

Hobbs, Nicholas, Perrin, James M., Ireys, Henry T., Moynihan, Linda Christie, and Shayne, May W. Chronically Ill Children in America: Background and Recommendations. Nashville, TN: Vanderbilt Institute for Public Policy Studies, 1983.

Hymovich, D. and R. Chamberlin. Child and Family Development. New York: McGraw-Hill Book Company, 1980.

International Diabetes Center, Learning to Live WELL With Diabetes. Minneapolis, MN: 1985.

Kubler-Ross, Elizabeth. On Death and Dying. New York: MacMillan, 1969.

Kushner, H.S. When Bad Things Happen to Good People. New York: Avon, 1981.

Leach, Penelope. Your Baby and Child: From Birth to Age Five. New York: Alfred A. Knopf, 1981.

Massie, Robert K. The Constant Shadow: Reflections on the Life of a Chronically Ill Child; in Hobbs and Perrin, 1985, 14–15.

McCollum, Audrey. The Chronically Ill Child: A Guide for Parents and Professionals. Boston: Little Brown & Co., 1981.

Miezio, Peggy Muller. Parenting Children with Disabilities. New York: Marcel Dekker, 1983.

Murphy, Albert T. Special Children, Special Parents: Personal Issues with Handicapped Children. Englewood Cliffs, NJ: Prentice-Hall, 1981.

PATHFINDER. How to Help Your Child. Eau Claire, WI: 1987.

Piaget, J. The Child's Concept of the World. New York: Humanities Press, 1951.

Pitzele, Sefra K. We Are Not Alone: Learning to Live with Chronic Illness. New York: Workman, 1986.

Resnick, Michael, et al. Minnesota Adolescent Health Survey. Minneapolis, MN: University of Minnesota, 1987.

Satter, Ellyn. Child of Mine: Feeding with Love and Good Sense. Palo Alto, CA: Bull Publishing Co., 1983.

Siminerio, Linda and Betschart, Jean. Children with Diabetes. New York: American Diabetes Association, 1986.

Travis, G. Chronic Illness in Children: Its Impact on Child and Family. Stanford, CA: Stanford University Press, 1976.

Turecki, Stanley. The Difficult Child. New York, Bantam Books, 1985.

Turnbull, H. Rutherford and Turnbull, Ann P. Parents Speak Out: Then and Now. Columbus, Ohio: Charles E. Merrill Publishing Co., 1985.

Wentworth, Elsie H. Listen to Your Heart: A Message to Parents of Handicapped Children. Boston: Houghton Mifflin, 1974.

Index

· ·

smoking, 108, 132
smoking, see also
   tobacco
soccer, 93
social worker, 155
spanking, 19, 33, 119,
   121
special education test-
   ing, 149
special education, 157
special events, 99
specialist(s), 68, 136,
   137, 139, 155
speech, 98
spiritual dogma, 129
spirituality, 9, 116
Stanford-Binet Intelli-
   gence (IQ) test, 160
stealing, 101
Steil, Dr. Lyman 112
step families, 26, 57
stepchildren, 57
stranger anxiety, 77,
   80
stress control, 9, 10,
   13, 15, 35, 70, 89, 98,
   124
stress response, 13
stress, 9, 10, 13, 15, 35,
   70, 89, 98, 124

stroke, 108
Strong Willed Child,
   The, 29
Subtreasury of Ameri-
   can Humor, 18
summer school, 100
superdad, 58
supermom, 58
superwoman syndrome,
   58
surgery, 76, 139
synagogue, 114
teachers, xiii
teenager(s), 104
time outs, 121
tobacco, xiii, 99, 108
tobacco, see also
   smoking
toddler stage, 79
toddler, xiii
toilet training, xiii, 79,
   82, 85, 88
tooth brushing, 88
trains, 95
transactional analysis,
   36
transportation, 110
tuberculosis, 2
tutoring, 149, 157

unconditional love, 65,
   77, 116
UNICEF, 133
University of Chicago,
   10
urinary frequency, 82
urination, 85
vacations, 59
Valentine's Day, 99
Vanderbilt University,
   ix
vision test(s), 157, 159
vision, 97
vocabulary, 90, 97
wages, 114
We Are Not Alone:
   Living with Chronic
   Illness, 1, 16
Wechsler Intelligence
   Scale for Children
   (WISC), 160
welfare, 112
wheelchairs, 154
Whitman, Walt, 105
Winter's Tale, 103
wisdom, 128
Wizard of Oz, 65
Your Child's Self-
   Esteem, 53

If you found this book helpful and would like more information on this and other related subjects, you may be interested in one or more of the following titles from our *Wellness and Nutrition Library.*

BOOKS

Diabetes 101: A Pure and Simple Guide for People Who Use Insulin (110 pages)
Expresslane Diet: (176 pages)
Retirement: New Beginnings, New Challenges, New Successes (140 pages)
Whole Parent/Whole Child: Raising a Child with a Chronic Illness (175 pages)
Diabetes: A Guide to Living Well (365 pages)
D.A.S.H. Diabetes . . . Actively Staying Healthy (160 pages)
Adult Braces in a Gourmet World (148 pages)
I Can Cope: Staying Healthy with Cancer (202 pages)
Managing Type II Diabetes (148 pages)
Managing the School Age Child with a Chronic Health Condition (350 pages)
Pass the Pepper Please (66 pages)
The Guiltless Gourmet (170 pages)
The Joy of Snacks (270 pages)
Fast Food Facts (56 pages)
Convenience Food Facts (188 pages)
Learning to Live Well With Diabetes (392 pages)
The Physician Within (170 pages)
Exchanges for All Occasions (250 pages)
Opening the Door to Good Nutrition (186 pages)

BOOKLETS & PAMPHLETS

Eating with Food Choices (40 pages)
A Guide to Healthy Eating (60 pages)
Diabetes & Alcohol (4 pages)
Diabetes & Exercise (20 pages)
Emotional Adjustment to Diabetes (16 pages)
A Step In Time: Diabetes Foot Care (18 pages)
Diabetes Record Book (68 pages)
Diabetes & Brief Illness (8 pages)
Diabetes & Impotence: A Concern for Couples (6 pages)
Adding Fiber to Your Diet (10 pages)
Gestational Diabetes: Guidelines for a Safe Pregnancy and Healthy Baby (24 pages)
Recognizing and Treating Insulin Reactions (4 pages)
Hypoglycemia (functional) (4 pages)

PROFESSIONAL SERIES
Manual of Clinical Nutrition (540 pages)
Simplified Learning Series—17 booklet preview packet
Diabetes Youth Curriculum: For working with young diabetics from age 6 to 16.

The *Wellness and Nutrition Library* is published by Diabetes Center, Inc. in Minneapolis, Minnesota, publishers of quality educational materials dealing with health, wellness, nutrition, diabetes, and other chronic illnesses. All our books and materials are available nationwide and in Canada through leading bookstores. If you are unable to find our books at your favorite bookstore contact us directly for a free catalog.

DCI Publishing, Inc.
P.O. Box 739
Wayzata, MN 55391